Transition to 21st Century Socialism in the European Union

Paul Cockshott, Allin Cottrell, Heinz Dieterich

This paper attempts to outline the economic steps that would be necessary to convert a capitalist economy like the EU into a socialist one. We examine the issue in very concrete terms and propose specific policy measures. The measures we propose differ significantly from the tradition of 20th century European Social Democracy.

Keynes famously remarked that practical political men, whether they be cautious or bold, found themselves unconsciously repeating the ideas of long dead economists. Politicians who advance neo-liberalism are, whether they know it or not, repeating the ideas of the reactionary Austrian economists Mises and Hayek. Socialist politicians purvey, in simplified form, the ideas of long dead Germanic Social Democratic economists such as Kautsky, Bernstein and Bauer.

1 Background

Historically, the dominant perspective on socialism has been that developed in the German Social Democratic Party in the years before the first world war. The SPD was the strongest and most influential party in the Socialist International and its ideas influenced other parties, including both the British Labour Party[1] and the European Communist Parties. Lih[2][3] has shown the extent to which the Leninism to which the latter subscribed was in fact just a re-labeling of classical German Social Democracy. We are used to see Social Democracy and Communism as very different, but the original distinguishing feature of Communism – that it sought power by preparing armed insurrection, was long ago abandoned by most communist political parties. This original communist principle has been retained only by Maoist parties in Asia and South America, all other left wing parties are in this sense Social Democrats.

When we use the word Social Democratic therefore we are refering to a tradition which existed prior to 1914. In the 1950s the original German Social Democrats abandoned their commitment to public ownership of the means of production, after which the term Social Democrat changed its popular meaning, and came to indicate a tendancy somewhere to the right of socialism. Socialists in the Labour Party in Britain and the Socialist Party in France counterposed themselves to this later meaning Social Democracy from the 1960s. We would argue however that so long as the Labour Party retiained its 1918 programatic commitment:

---

1   We would argue that by the mid 1950s the British Labour Party was more classically Social Democratic than the then SPD.
2   We elaborate on this in our book [1, 2].

"To secure for the workers by hand or by brain the full fruits of their industry and the most equitable distribution thereof that may be possible upon the basis of the common ownership of the means of production, distribution and exchange, and the best obtainable system of popular administration and control of each industry or service."

Once this programmatic commitment was dropped by Blair, the LP ceased to have any connection with Social Democracy in its original sense.

It was not until the 1940s that European (as opposed to Russian) Social Democracy got an opportunity to try changing the economic system. The UK, the newly formed GDR, Czechoslovakia, Poland and other countries embarked on an economic transformation that had certain common characteristics:

- Key industries were taken into state ownership.
- Education and healthcare became free state services.
- Publicly owned housing became the dominant form of new construction.
- Attempts were made, either by confiscation or by inheritance taxation, to diminish the great landed estates.
- The state attempted to follow a policy of full employment.

There were obviously differences. In Eastern Germany and Czechoslovakia agriculture was largely brought under state control whereas in the UK and Poland state farms played a much more minor role, with intervention in the UK being mainly through state marketing boards. We will concentrate for a while on the UK, both because the authors are particularly familiar with it, and also because UK economic policy had a big international impact.

The process of nationalisation of industry did not go so far in the UK as in Eastern Europe, but even there by the late 1970s the state owned among other things

- the system of energy production and supply: coal, oil, gas, nuclear power and hydro electricity;
- much of the transport system: roads, railways, buses, airlines, airports, ports;
- the communication system: radio, TV, post, telephones;
- the majority of the housing stock; and
- many heavy industries: steel, shipbuilding, aircraft construction, car production.

However the old property owning classes were not expropriated in the West and many sections of industry remained in private hands. A reliance was placed on inheritance taxes to eventually expropriate the property owning classes. Tax avoidance meansures by the wealthy meant that these taxes had less effect than hoped. The existence of such a large state sector, in combination with a strong trade union movement, had, by the mid-1970s, seriously threatened the continued viability of the remaining capitalist sections of the economy, resulting in a major crisis of profitability. There was a lively debate within British Social Democracy about what to do. Should the crisis be resolved by more vigorous state controls over prices and incomes whilst retaining the existing private sector? Should it be resolved by extending state ownership and using a new state investment bank to fund investment?

The Labour Party was effectively paralysed with indecision and was replaced in 1979 by a radical neo-liberal government headed by Mrs Thatcher. This reversed many of the social democratic changes made after 1945 with the explicit aim of returning to a classical liberal capitalist economy.

Within a decade, neo-liberal policy had become dominant not only in Britain but in all of the European countries in which classical Social Democratic economic policies had been most influential. Paradoxically, the Federal Republic of Germany, in which Social Democratic economics had made less inroads, was one of the last countries to move to neo-liberalism.

Now, in the 21st century and in face of the most serious crisis of capitalism since the 1930s, there is an historic opportunity to reassert the original ideals and objectives of the socialist and democratic workers movements But this cannot simply be a repetition of the past. In this proposal we try to develop an alternative that differs in the following ways from past European Socialism:

1. We do not place the nationalisation of industry at the center of our concerns; instead we emphasise a positive assertion of the rights of labour to the full value added.
2. We propose a radical restructuring of monetary policy to move the whole economy towards a non-money 'equivalence economy' based on working time.
3. We envisage transition as taking place not at the level of the nation state but within a democratised European Union.

Let us summarise key features of our conception of mature socialism:

1. The economy is based on the deliberate and conscious application of the labour theory of value as developed by Adam Smith and Karl Marx. It is a model in which consumer goods are priced in terms of the hours and minutes of labour it took to make them, and in which each worker is paid labour credits for each hour worked. The consistent application of this principle eliminates economic exploitation.
2. Industry is publicly owned, run according to a plan and not for profit. Retail enterprises for example, work on a break-even rather than profit making basis. We envisage the transition to publicly owned enterprises as being a gradual process that will occur after rather than before the abolition of the wages system.
3. Decisions are taken democratically, at local, national and Union levels. This applies in particular to decisions about the level of taxation and state expenditure. Such democratic decision making is vital to prevent the replacement of private exploitation with exploitation by the state.

In addition we take seriously Marx's aphorism that the liberation of the working classes must be the work of the working classes themselves. This is reflected in our advocacy of direct participative democracy rather than cabinet or party government and also affects our philosophy of how a transition to socialism has to take place. Instead of the old Social Democratic emphasis on the direct action of the state in nationalising and taking over private companies, we advocate the establishment of positive legal rights for labour. These rights will, when collectively exercised by workers, bring to an end the exploitation of labour by capital.

2 Money and exploitation

The European economy will still based on money at the point at which the socialist movement comes to power. In Capital, Marx showed how money was at the root of the evils of capitalism. The essence of capitalism is to start out with a sum of money at the beginning of the year and end up with a larger sum at the end. Marx denoted this by M->M' where M might be £"£" 1,000,000 for example and M'=£"£" 2,000,000.

Because capitalists have more money than working people, they can use this money to hire workers to work for wages. As Adam Smith pointed out, in any bargain over the price of their labour, workers are in a weaker position than employers. Their wages are much less than the value they create during the working week. Since the capitalists can sell the product for more value than they paid out in wages, the capitalists become richer and richer while workers stay as poor as ever. This process is the root cause of the difference between rich and poor.

On top of this there is a secondary form of exploitation that allows capitalists to increase their wealth: lending money at interest. This process allows the money-lender to get richer year by year by doing absolutely nothing. This process has become increasingly important as a form of exploitation within the developed capitalist countries. The extension of credit in the last 30 years means that the great bulk of the working class and lower middle classes and are in debt, exploited by the banks and credit card companies. The neo liberal policies of the last decades have widened the gap between rich and poor. A large part of societies income is now concentrated in very few hands. The rich tend to save a large part of their income. In consequence there would have been insufficient consumer demand to keep the economy going without the extension of consumer credit. The system needs employees to consume, but to run at a profit employees can only get a portion of the value created. The wealthy then lend workers back part of the value they created. But this process is self limiting, eventually the debt burden can grow no further.

In addition to supporting exploitation, the a monetary market economy is incompatible with the planned use of resources to meet social needs. In the EU — unlike, for example, the USSR — the supply of most goods and services is regulated by the market. This is not entirely a bad thing: it does, to a limited extent, allow supply to be adjusted to match people's wants. The drawback is that the provision of goods and services is systematically biased towards the wishes and desires of the rich. The EU currently lacks the mechanisms by which the structure of the economy as a whole can be regulated in a conscious social way to meet the challenge of climate change and to equitably meet the needs of all citizens.

3 How to effect the transformation

We will now shift the focus to specific policy measures. We will present these one by one and while explaining how each measure helps to achieve the broader objectives we have described.

3.1 Monetary reform

European monetary policy is dominated by the European Central Bank (ECB). This institution, operating outside of any democratic control, is charged with ensuring the monetary conditions for the continued reproduction of European capitalism. The removal of the bank from democratic control, and the imposition of strict anti-inflationary policies, represent one of the key victories of late 20th century liberalism. Of itself, inflation is not necessarily against the interests of the poor and working classes, provided that wages keep up with prices. The people who are hit hardest by inflation are the rentier class whose holdings of money and interest bearing assets depreciate. Since these people are opponents of socialism anyway, a socialist government might not worry about any financial loss these people suffer, were it not for the other social effects of inflation.

Uncertainty about future prices can lead to a social psychology of instability leading to a loss of confidence in the social order. For this if for no other reason, it is desirable that a socialist government in Europe follow a policy of price stability. Indeed, our proposals to replace money with labour vouchers are tantamount to a long term policy of declining prices.

Given an objective to establish a socialist economy based on the equivalent payment of labour, monetary reform is a step towards this goal. We suggest that the ECB be placed under a legal obligation to maintain *a stable value of the currency in terms of labour*. A prototype for this could be the successful monetary policy of the British Labour Government after 1996. At that time the government placed monetary policy under a committee of expert economists (the Monetary Policy Committee) rather than politicians, and gave them a clear legal obligation to achieve a particular target rate of inflation. One might have expected this policy to be severely deflationary, but it was not. In part because, unlike the European Central Bank, the committee are legally obliged to avoid both deflation and inflation[3].

Where our proposal differs from British policy is in the goal it sets — namely, fixing the value of the Euro in terms of labour rather than in terms of the cost of living index — and in advocating a democratic composition of the Value Policy Committee which should control the ECB.

The aim would be to fix the value of the Euro in terms of the average number of hours of embodied labour that an hour of labour will purchase. There exist well established techniques using national input output tables by which the equivalence of money to labour time can be calculated. Our colleague Stahmer explains these. If in 2009 an hour was worth roughly 30 Euros and the VPC wanted to stabilise this, they would have to adjust the issue of Euros up or down to ensure that the exchange of embodied labour against Euros remained constant.

Capitalist central banks try to control inflation by adjusting the interest rate. If inflation is too high, they raise interest rates. The effect is to choke off investment, reduce demand, and so reduce inflationary pressures. If interest is banned, how is the price level to be regulated? or, in the light of what we said earlier how would the Value Policy Committee ensure that the value of the Euro in terms of labour was held steady?

An alternative control mechanism would be to adjust the overall volume of loans and/or the maximum term for which loans are made. The state bank could set volume targets and maximum durations for loans. For example, if the Value Policy Committee thought the value of the currency was in danger of falling it could limit the availability of loans or shorten the period for which loans could be had. If loan periods were reduced from 10 year to 5 years, then monthly repayments rise, just as happens with interest rate rises today.

Another means of regulating prices is tax policy. Paper money, like the Euro, is inherently worthless, just printed paper. It has value imputed to it, from the fact that the state (or a confederation of states) will accept its own currency for tax debts. The fact that people need money to pay their taxes, forces them to value it. If governments tax less than they spend, the money stock will rise leading to inflation. The second way to regulate prices during the transition to socialism is thus to fine tune tax levels.

---

3   We would not fully endorse these objectives. In particular the failure of the MCP's remit to include anything about the balance of trade, certainly contributed to a terrible build up of overseas debt.

The reasons for the goal are :
1. As labour productivity rises, a Euro fixed in terms of hours of labour will be able to buy more each year, cheapening the cost of living.
2. Once the value of the Euro has been stabilised in terms of labour value the labour value of Euro notes should be printed on them in hours and minutes. This step would be an act of revolutionary pedagogy. It would reveal clearly to employees just how the existing system cheats them. Suppose a worker puts in a working week of 45 hours and gets back Euros and sees that the hours printed on them amount to only 20 hours, then she will become aware that she is being cheated out of 25 hours each week. This will act to raise socialist consciousness, and create favourable public opinion for other socialist measures.
3. As a final stage the Euro would be renamed and redefined in terms of work time, and would cease to be a transferable physical currency. People would have electronic credits measured in, say, European Standard Hours, which would be redeemable against goods containing the same number of hours of work, but which could not be used for private speculative transactions.

Instead of just having a committee of economists charged with regulating the value of the Euro, the principle of participative democracy implies that the Value Policy Committee should be made up both of economists and members of the European public selected on a jury basis.

The Value Policy Committee would have to commission surveys of how much work was being done in different industries, and how much monetary value added there was in these industries, in order to guide its stabilisation policy. The definition of monetary value added would be the same as that currently used to compute Value Added Tax.

3.2 Reform of accounting and pressure for fair prices

All firms currently have to prepare money accounts, The state should make it a condition of their accounts being approved, that they also produce labour-time accounts and that they mark on all products their labour content.

Initially firms need not be legally obliged to sell their commodities at their true values. They could attempt to sell them for a price that is higher or lower than the true value. But since consumers can now see when they are being overcharged, they will tend to avoid companies that sell goods at above their true value. This will put psychological and consumer pressure on companies that are overcharging. This too will be an act of socialist mass pedagogy.

At an early stage in transition, before all goods have their labour values printed on their price tags, firms will have to impute labour values to the goods they purchase using the printed exchange rate between Euros and labour hours. They will add to the labour value of their inputs the number of hours of work that are performed by their employees to get a labour value for the final product.

At the level of National and Union accounts the EU should also move towards having a dual system of accounts, labour accounts alongside money accounts. Because, at the level of EU economic policy, there are many issues on which labour accounts would be more informative than money accounts. For instance in estimating the budget levels required to achieve full employment, this is much more readily done if one is comparing expenditure in labour with known labour reserves in the form of unemployment. In addition physical input output tables, and tables denominated in carbon dioxide outputs would be required. Money accounts hide the fact that what government economic policy really does is re-allocate society's labour. Money is the veil behind which real labour allocation occurs.

3.3 Enshrine the rights of labour in law

Scientific evidence shows that in the capitalist world the money value of goods is overwhelmingly determined by their labour contents. Studies find that for most economies the correlation between labour values and prices is 95% or above. So Adam Smith's scientific hypothesis that labour was the source of value has now been statistically verified. This scientific fact should be incorporated in law.

3.3.1 The right not to be exploited

European law should recognise that labour is the sole source of value and that in consequence workers, and their Unions, will have a claim in law against their employers if they are paid less than the full value of their labour. If we consider the previous measures and the educational effect that would follow from them, it should be relatively easy to pass a referendum on such a law.

Following such a law being passed, there would be a huge wave of worker activism as workers sought to end the cheating and deceit to which they and their ancestors had been subjected. It would also bring about a very large increase in real wages, cementing support for the socialist government.

The employing class, on the other hand would see sharp fall in their unearned incomes. Employers who were active factory managers would of course still be legally entitled to be paid for the hours that they put in managing the firm, just like any other employee.

Note that at this stage the establishment of the right to full value created would not mean the elimination of wage differentials. A legal right to the full value created would be a collective right of employees as a whole within a company. Such a system would certainly create strong moral pressures towards the equalisation of rates of pay, but the process by which this came about would be a matter for future collective bargaining and future civil rights legislation. Just as there is now legislation against gender discrimination in pay, a future European society is likely to legislate against other forms of pay inequality.

The tribunals to which such claims were brought would have to be dominated by juries rather than professional judges. Juries drawn from the population at large are likely to be less influenced by the special interests of the employing class than are judges whose social position is close to that of the employing class.

3.3.2 The right to industrial democracy

The emphasis above is on the state enabling the workers to act collectively to prevent exploitation. If unions won court actions giving employees the full value that they created, then there is a danger that some firms would attempt to close down and fire workers rather than continue in business. Thus legislation aimed at protecting the rights of labour would have to include the right, after a suitable ballot of employees, for employees to elect the majority of the board of any company.

The cumulative effect of the measures outlined so far would be to substantially abolish capitalist exploitation in the workplace at least in the short term. There will be long term difficulties if other measures are not taken, and we shall examine these later.

3.4 Eliminating other forms of exploitation

In addition to the exploitation of employees by employers, there are other forms of unearned incomes, the most important of which are interest and rent.

3.4.1 Usury

Interest, the getting of money from money itself, was regarded for thousands of years as sinful. Philosophers like Aristotle condemned it. Papal encyclicals banned it. Islamic law still forbids it in Muslim countries. But in capitalist countries, such was the social power of the banks and other money lenders that this moral objection came to be forgotten.

In capitalist countries which were undergoing very rapid industrialisation, for instance, Japan in the 1950s or 1960s, lending money at interest did serve a necessary economic purpose, since it allowed peoples savings to be channelled, via the banks, to fund industrialisation. But once a country has industrialised, firms finance most of their investment from internal profits. Indeed they normally have more profit than they know how to invest. Instead of borrowing from the banks, industrial firms run a financial surplus, and they themselves lend to the banks. The banks now channel the financial surplus of firms into loans to consumers, or to governments. Lending at interest looses the temporary progressive function that it had during industrialisation and reverts to being what morality and religion originally condemned : usury.

Socialism abolishes interest as a form of income. It has no class of rentiers people who do no work but just live off the interest on their money. So it is clear that at some point, that a government seriously intent upon socialism has to pass legislation banning the lending of money at interest. It could specify, for instance, that interest on debt could not be enforced in the civil courts. It could impose severe criminal penalties on those who used threats of harm to extort interest.

Before moving to a step such as this, a socialist government needs to put in place replacements for the economic functions still served by lending, and charging interest.

3.4.2 Rent

Rent is another type of exploitation. Socialists regard it as immoral since the owner of land enriches himself, not by his own labour, but by the labour of others combined with the niggardliness of nature. Rent is however an inevitable phenomenon in a commodity producing society. If there is some product, be it crude oil, or corn, the efficiency of whose production depends on the land being used, then rent incomes will arise.

In a socialist economy all rent income should accrue to the state and be used for the good of the community. Socialist states have usually nationalised land, but have not always charged a rent for using the land. In the case of mineral extraction this made no difference, since this was done by state enterprises and rent would just have been a fictitious transfer between sections of the state. Failure to charge agricultural rents to farms will, however, accentuate differences in income between fertile and less fertile agricultural regions.

It is a moot point whether land nationalisation would be popular today in Europe. An economic alternative, which over the long term would produce a similar effect, would be to introduce a land tax on the rentable value of land. This is an old populist objective, originally proposed by Henry George. The threshold for the tax could be set high enough to ensure that small farmers paid nothing or only a token amount, but for larger more fertile estates it could be set at a level that would confiscate the greater part of rent revenue. The effect on large landowners would be to deprivethem of their unearned income and making it available for communal uses If they refused it would be tax evasion but it is ideologically harder for the likes of the Duke of Atholl to mount a campaign to justify tax evasion than it is to mount one to justify resistance to expropriation.

3.5 Investment

It will still be necessary to fund new investments. During the crisis of 2008 it has been necessary for some European states to take control of large parts of the banking system. From this basis it is clear that investment could in principle be funded by interest free loans from publicly controlled banks. In a time of recession however, it becomes important to ensure the availability of credit, so that even capitalist governments have to impose controls on the banking system. But if this is not done with care, the resulting expansion of the money stock will lead to the type of suppressed inflation which occurred in the USSR.

Investment on credit is based on the illusion that you can push the cost of investment into the future. Whilst this can be true for an individual borrower, for society as a whole, today's investment has to be made using today's labour. As a society we can not get future generations to travel back in time in order to do work for us. Socialist economies should thus rely predominantly on tax revenue to fund investment.

3.6 Debt and the credit crisis

Mature capitalist economies have an inbuilt potential for slump because the property owning classes tend to have more income than they can readily spend. In the early stages of industrial development this is channeled through the banks to finance real investment. As reserves of labour get used up, increasingly capital intensive investment is faced with a law of diminishing returns and becomes less profitable. If investment is insufficient to balance saving, a slump is initiated.

The Keynesian solution to this was to tax the property owning classes and spend the proceeds on public projects to keep the economy buoyant. The neo-liberal approach since 1980 has been to cut tax on the propertied classes, whilst at the same time greatly easing the rules on consumer credit. Both solutions worked for a while.

The credit crisis of 2008 marked a turning point for the neo-liberal model. Credit had been extended so far that the ratio of debt to real income became unsustainable. The result was a general banking crisis. Instead of allowing banks to fail, the state bailed them out. Governments expressed relief that their action prevented a cascading collapse, but the cost was a growth in public debt unprecedented in peacetime. Was any other policy available?

There was an alternative policy. The failing banks could simply have been allowed to fail. The deposit guarantee schemes were generous. Only a small minority of bank customers held more than the guaranteed deposit. The majority would not have lost anything had the banks failed. Most customers have only modest amounts of cash, but a few very rich customers have tens of millions deposited. To them, the deposit guarantees were practically worthless.

The trillion-Euro public bailout was done to protect the claims of these few very rich depositors. Had all deposits above the the guarantee vanished, the class system would be threatened. For, Adam Smith said, what is money but the power to command the labour of others? Billions in a bank account play the role of a patent of nobility under feudalism. Modern Grand Dukes like like Lakshmi Mittal or the Albrechts' have their titles on a bank's hard drive rather than parchment, but they like their predecessors, still command the lives and labour of hundreds of thousands.

Had the banks all closed down, credit card and cheque purchases would become impossible. But instead of allowing them to fail, a Jubilee could have been declared. It would have declared all debts incurred prior to Day Zero legally invalid, excepting modest guaranteed deposits. Those toiling to meet mortgage and credit card debt would have been liberated. The taxpayer would have been freed from the crushing burden of the national debt, and surprisingly, the banks would have become super-solvent. Their liabilities would have shrunk relative to their cash reserves. Industry would have remained privately owned. But the abolition of debt, which has been a radical measure since antiquity, would have hit the aristocracy of money the way the French revolution hit the aristocracy of land.

The Russians did it after 1917, and shortly later, the German Social Democrats achieved a similar effect via hyper-inflation. Today, some governments have veered towards the German 1920's course: printing money to pay for the huge debts they have taken on. The inflation that results could hit small and large depositors alike. The alternative of abolishing debts serves to polarise political opinion against the peoples' main enemy—the rentier interest—whilst benefiting the majority.

3.7 State Finance

This brings us onto the general topic of state finance. Socialist economies typically have a higher level of state expenditure than capitalist ones at a comparable level of economic development. It is essential that the state has an efficient revenue raising mechanism, with taxes that are easy to collect and difficult to avoid. Social democratic states like Sweden relied mainly on income taxes along with an efficient civil service. The USSR relied upon turnover taxes on industry and on profits earned by state firms. Which of these models of tax revenue should be used is one of the major strategic issues that has to be faced by as an economy moves towards a socialism.

We argue that the Soviet model of taxation had several drawbacks, which, in the long run, contributed to the final collapse of the Soviet socialist economy.
a. The use of indirect taxation, such as turnover or value added taxes, and a fortiori reliance on profit income, puts the state in the position of being a collective capitalist vis a vis the workers.
b. The use of indirect taxation has also traditionally been opposed by socialists as this is a regressive rather than progressive form of taxation.

c. It resulted in a distorted price structure that systematically undervalued labour, to the detriment of economic efficiency.
d. Reliance on the profit of state industry is a hidden form of revenue, which is not easily amenable to democratic control.

We therefore strongly advocate a reliance on income and asset taxes rather than indirect taxes. The tax basis of the Union should be switched from VAT to progressive income and asset taxes. The European Parliament should be able to adjust the tax rates paid to the Union, subject to gaining a majority in a Union-wide referendum.

At the moment the parliament can not raise revenues on its own account, a fundamental requirement for a genuinely democratic assembly. But given the suspicion of the Union that exists, it would be unwise to allow parliament to introduce or change taxes without popular support.

1. Either the parliament or citizens initiatives should be able to propose new Union taxes such as income taxes, customs duties or property taxes provided that these pass a popular vote.
2. The broad headings of the budget should be subject to popular vote.
3. The EU central bank should be subject to the parliament.

4 EU Democratisation

The split in authority and economic power between the EU and the nation states has at least partially blocked the road to the old social democratic / Keynesian means of dealing with recessions. Constraints on budgetary policy, lack of control over the currency and capital flows prevent nation states from following classic Keynesian policies. At the same time the EU itself lacks the budget or the power to substitute for the nation states in this situation. A consequence is the absence of a political form in which the labour movement of Europe can express itself in classical social democratic politics.

In the absence of classical social democratic politics you do not get the clear constitution of a European employee class, since a class cannot be constituted outside of a political party in the broad sense of the word.

Consequently we argue that it is necessary for the labour movements of Europe to take on board their own democratic version of European internationalism, since neither the technocrats of the EU itself nor the propertied classes of Europe are capable of doing this.

The proposed democratisation is a return to the original principles of European democracy in ancient Greece[4] seeking to eliminate the Roman Republican elements which were instituted after the French revolution. At its heart must be the principle of popular sovereignty, and genuinely representative democracy.

1. Popular sovereignty being enshrined in the right of initiative and referendum on a whole Europe-wide basis on any issue for which a sufficient quorum of signatures, spread across enough countries can be obtained. This direct participation in binding votes as European citizens rather than citizens of the nations would constitute the Union as a real focus of politics. The right of initiative would encourage the formation of Union wide campaigns and movements. It could be exploited immediately by the trades union movement of Europe and would give them an impetus to unite in practice.
2. We are taking this consciously Jacobin position in favour of strong democratic center, becaus only that has the power to confront internationally organised big business and big finance.
3. We argue that the parliament be a citizens' body, not a body of highly paid elite politicians. At the very least we argue for the members to face elections annually and for the limitation of office to a maximum of 2 years to prevent the formation of a class of professional politicians divorced from the population. Half of the parliament should be chosen by lot rather than elected as present on a party list system. This again aims to increase citizen participation, across all classes and genders.
4. The EU commission should be selected from and by the parliament rather than being party placemen.
5. The parliament can legislate on any subject and if faced by a veto in the council of ministers can call a citizens vote to override the nation state representatives.

---

4 We of course know that women and slaves could not vote in Athens, but until the early 20th century women and workers could not vote in Europe under the parliamentary system. We are obviously not advocating a regression to slavery and patriarchy. What we are saying is that current EU states derived their constitutional model from the Roman Republic via the French Revolution, and as such conciously adopted a state form that was optimal to the rule of the propertied classes. It was for this reason that Ancient Greece faced the treaon of its propertied classes when invaded by Roman Imperialism. The Republic was seen then and now as the ideal form of rule by the wealthy.

5 The ordering of measures

The measures above undermine what are important functional components of capitalism and there would be adverse consequences if alternative mechanisms were not put into place.

Ending the production of profit by paying workers the full value they create would make employment unprofitable. There is a danger under these circumstances that capitalists would find it more profitable to leave their money in the bank and earn interest on it than use it to employ workers. It is important that the payment of interest be abolished prior to introducing the right to the full value of labour.

It would be necessary to introduce the right for employees to vote for their firm to be co-managed by a committee having a clear majority of employees on it, to stop asset stripping and closing of the now unprofitable firms.

After this phase of transition the economy would still be capitalist, but the ownership role of individual capitalists would be greatly reduced. The most serious economic disruption would have been to the financial sector where the profitability of stockbroking and investment banking firms would drastically decline. But this decline would be manageable, being no worse than the structural changes to many heavy industries that occurred during the last 20 years.

A second phase of transition involves the development of the capacity for detailed planning - setting up of the administrative system, establishment of the democratic control mechanisms and construction of the computer networks and software that would be required to carry out the sort of planning discussed in our book [1]. Initially these plans would be indicative, becoming mandatory as the system bedded down.

6 Conclusion

We have outlined a model for the conversion of EU type economies that differs from the tradition deriving from German Social Democracy. The three stages of transition are shown below as a table.

Stage	Money	Property/rights	Coordination	Tax
1	Euro notes	Capital right to	Market	Indirect and direct
(now)		value added		
2	Euro notes Tied	Labour right to	Market +	Direct +
	to labour	value added,	public banks	Property tax
	Debt cancelled	no interest		
3	Euro Labour	Labour right to	Consumer goods	Direct taxes +
	accounts	value added	market + cybernetic	democratic
	non circulating	no interest	coordination	budget

Stage 1 outlines the current situation. Stage 2 the situation whilst the conversion measures we describe in the paper are being applied. Stage 3 is the situation described Towards a New Socialism.

Unlike the classic social democratic process, there is no distinct stage of nationalisation of firms with the attendant issue of whether there is to be compensation or not. Instead, there is a basic change to the framework of company law so that labour rather than capital acquires the right to value added. There is then no need for the state either to confiscate or compensate shareholders. The situation would be analogous to the 13th amendment to the US constitution, which abolished slavery without compensating the slave owners. We are proposing that the Union similarly abolish wage slavery. Share holders could still own shares in firms, but they would have no right to obtain an income from them.

We are conscious of the fact that this New Historical Project of a postcapitalist civilization is a long and complex process that has to be resolved gradually, democratically and with the concurrence of all human beings who want to live in an ethical and democratic world society. But even the largest process begins with a tiny first step. We want this program to be that tiny first step and invite all of you to participate in its discussion and evolution in order to achieve a better life for all and the preservation of the planet.

References

[1] Paul Cockshott and Allin Cottrell.
Towards a New Socialism, volume Nottingham.
Bertrand Russell Press, 1993.

[2] W.P. Cockshott and A. Cottrell.
Alternativen aus dem Rechner.
PapyRossa, 2006.

[3] L.T. Lih and V.I. Lenin.
Lenin rediscovered: What is to be done? in context.
Brill Academic Pub, 2006.

A defence of socialism in the XXI century

Allin Cottrell and Paul Cockshott

Abstract

This is a paper originally presented at a conference 'New Historical Project' held in Quito in May 2003. Extended and updated in 2008. It elaborates on the vision of socialism presented in cursory form in the transition programme earlier in this document.

Introduction

Fifty years ago there was little doubt in the minds of socialists that planning was way of the future. This was borne out by the rapid advance of the planned economies, which with Sputnik and Gagarin seemed to outpace the muddled inefficiency of capitalist economies. Today of course the picture looks different.

In the face of the collapse of Soviet power at the end of the 80s, left wing authors seemed to have no ready response.

In fact, however, the very advances in information technology that are taken to symbolise the triumph of the market, hold even more potential for a rational and democratic socialism. This fact promise, is we think, now beginning to be understood by the movement for economic democracy.

Since the late 80s we have been arguing that there is an intellectually coherent and practical alternative to the philosophy of neo-liberalism. Our basic proposals can be laid out quite simply, although we ask the reader to bear in mind that we do not have space here for the necessary refinements, qualifications and elaborations (these are developed at length in Cockshott and Cottrell, 1993). In schematic form the proposals are as follows.

Thesis 1. *The collapse of previously existing socialism was due to identifiable causes embedded in its economic mechanism, but which are not inherent in all possible socialisms.*

Thesis 2. *Marxist economic theory, in conjunction with information technology provide the basis on which a viable socialist economic program can be advanced.*

Thesis 3. *The socialist movement has never developed a correct constitutional program. In particular it has accepted the misconception that elections are a democratic form.*

1 Historical failings

> The collapse of previously existing socialism was due to identifiable causes embedded in its economic mechanism, but which are not inherent in all possible socialisms.

We will examine some of the well known contradictions within the economics of previously existing socialism. The argument that these are not inherent in any socialism will be advanced in section 2.

Elaboration 1.1. *The mechanism for the extraction of a surplus product progressively collapsed resulting in inadequate investment.*

Marxist economics views the method of extracting a surplus product as being the distinguishing feature of a mode of production.

> The specific economic form, in which unpaid surplus labour is pumped out of the direct producers determines the relationship of rulers and ruled, as it grows directly out of production itself and, in turn, reacts upon it as a determining element. Upon this, however, is founded the entire formation of the economic community which grows up out of the production relations themselves, thereby simultaneously its specific political form. It is always the direct relationship of the owners of the conditions of production to the direct producers - a relation naturally corresponding to a definite stage in the development of the methods of labour and thereby its social productivity, - which reveals the innermost secret, the hidden basis of the entire social structure, and with it the political form of the relation of sovereignty and dependence, in short, the corresponding specific form of state. *See MARX 1972,p 791*

In a socialist economy the extraction of a surplus product takes place by means of **a politically determined division of the material product between consumer goods and other products in the state plan**. This is socialism's " innermost secret, the hidden basis of the entire social structure ".

Its system of extracting a surplus is quite different from under capitalism in the following respects:

- The division of the product is determined directly in material terms rather then indirectly as a result of exchange relations.

- The division is determined centrally rather than through numerous local bargains over the price of labour power, hours worked etc.

- The actual level of money wages is irrelevant because the supplies of consumer goods are predetermined in the plan. Higher money wages do not necessarily result in increased real wages. Besides which a large part of the real wage is in the form of free or subsidised goods.

This form of extraction rises out of the highly integrated and socialised character of production under socialism. From it is developed the absolute necessity of individual factories being subordinated to the center, and the comparative irrelevance of their individual profitablility. Following on it determines the centralised character of the state and the impossibility of local authorities having an autonomous disposition over resources. All these are invariant characteristics of socialism.

This innermost secret determines the relationship of rulers and ruled as follows; consider two possibilities, either the rulers and the ruled are distinct groups, or they are one and the same.

If, as in hitherto exisiting socialism, they are distinct, then whoever controls the planning authority is both the effective owner of the means of production, and a ruler. These rulers (in practice have the central committee of the communist party), though often venal, can not fulfill their social function by the shameless bourgeois pursuit of self interest. They are compelled instead, to take on the highly social and public role, of so organising the political and ideological life of the society, as to ensure compliance with the plan. One of the most effective ways of doing this is through the cult of a charismatic leader, backed to a greater or lesser extent by state terror.

Personality cults, in which the leader is presented as the General Will incarnate are no accident, but an efficient adaptation to the contradictory demands of a socialist mode of production (which dictates the dominance of political over civil society), combined with institutions of representative government.

Some readers may protest at this point: it is bad enough that we unblushingly characterize the Leninist system as socialist, but how can we say that it had a representative government?

Representative government selects certain humans, commonly called politicians, to stand in for, or represent, others in the process of political decision making. This is just what the Leninist party does in power. It acts as a representative of the working class and takes political decisions on its behalf. As such it is no less representative a form of government than parliamentary government, there are differences over who is represented and how they are represented, but the representative principle remains the same: decisions are not taken by those affected but are monopolized by a group of professional rulers, whose edicts are legitimated in terms of some representative function. Selection of such rulers by multiple party elections can not diminish their representative character nor abolish the distinction between rulers and ruled.

The contradictory character of socialist representative government is banally evident. The representatives of the proletariat, through their control of the plan, and thus the method by which unpaid surplus labour is pumped out of the direct producers, become effective controllers, *pro tem*, of the means of production. As such their individual class position is transformed and their ability to go on representing the proletariat, compromised.

Only if the distinction between ruler and ruled is abolished, when the masses themselves decide all major questions through institutions of participatory democracy does the totalitarian inner secret at the heart of socialism cease to be contradictory. Only when the masses in referenda decide the disposition of their collective social labour : how much is to go on defence, how much on health, how much on consumer goods etc, can the political life of socialism cease to be a fraud.

But to return to the question of surplus extraction. Under socialism this is an inherently totalitarian process, a subordination of the parts to the whole, the factory to the plan, the individual to the collective. Production is not for private gain but for the totality of society. Under a system of participatory democracy, this totalitarian conformism might take on a Swiss democratic rather than German fascist air, but it would be no less real.

Gorbachov undermined the whole surplus extraction process by attacking the totalitarian principle. One of his first measures was to allow factories to retain the greater part of their profit. At a stroke, he introduced an antagonistic bourgeois principle of surplus extraction: the pursuit of profit by individual enterprises. He threw the whole system into chaos.

The government, deprived of its main form of revenue, resorted to the printing press. The result was hyperinflation.

The factories had extra money, but, since the division of the social product was still determined by the plan, could not act as private firms would and convert this new money into productive capital. The socialist system of surplus extraction was sabotaged without a bourgeois one to replace it, and the economy spiraled into an inflationary decline.

Elaboration 1.2. *Previously existing socialism was limited by a deficient system of economic calculation.*

This point is made by all right wing critics. They point out, with justification, that the price system operating in the USSR made rational economic calculation impossible. Numerous anecdotes tell of this:

> Here is one of many examples. Some time ago it was decided to adjust the prices of cotton and grain in the interests of cotton growing, to establish more accurate prices for grain sold to the cotton growers, and to raise the prices of cotton delivered to the state. Our business executives and planners submitted a proposal on this score which could not but astound members of the Central Committee, since it suggested fixing the price of a ton of grain at practically the same level as a ton of cotton, and, moreover, the price of a ton of grain was taken as equivalent to that of a ton of baked bread. In reply to the remarks of the members of the Central Committee that the price of a ton of bread must be much higher than that of a ton of grain, because of the additional expense of milling and baking, and that cotton was generally much dearer than grain was also borne out by their prices in the world market, the authors of the proposal could find nothing coherent to say.

So wrote Stalin in April 1952 [Stalin 1952], but some 40 years later, pricing policy had improved so little that Gorbachov could cite the example of pigs being fed bread by collective farmers, because the price of bread was lower than that of grain.

When the relative prices of things differs systematically from their relative costs of production, it becomes impossible for people to chose cost effective methods of production. This produces a general decline in economic efficiency.

Elaboration 1.3. *Unlike capitalism, previously existing socialism lacked an inbuilt mechanism to economise on the use of labour, and thus to raise its productivity.*

The fundamental economic justification of any new production technology has to be its ability to produce things with less effort than before.

Only by the constant application of such inventions throughout the economy can we gain more free time to devote either to leisure or to the satisfaction of new and more sophisticated tastes. This implies that in socialist production workers must seek always to economise on time. Time is, as Adam Smith said, our original currency by which we purchase from nature all our wants and necessities, a moment of it needlessly squandered is lost for ever. A socialist system will only be historically superior to capitalism if it proves better at husbanding time.

The wealth of capitalist societies is of course unevenly divided, but its inbuilt tendency to advance the productivity of labour underpins the continuing progressive role of capitalist economic relations. Had capitalism lost this potential, as some Marxists believed in the 1930's then it would long ago have lost out in competition with the Soviet block.

In a capitalist economy, manufacturers are driven by the desire for profit to try to minimise costs. These costs include wages. Firms often introduce new technology in order to cut the workforce and reduce labour costs. Although this use of technology is frequently against the direct interest of workers, who loose their jobs, it is to the ultimate benefit of society. For it is through these economies in labour that the living standards of the society is raised. The benefits of technical change are unevenly spread, the employer stands to gain more than the employee, but in the end, it is upon its ability to foster technological improvements that capitalism's claim to be a progressive system is based. The need to accept new labour saving technology is generally recognised within the Trades Unions, who seek only to regulate the terms of its introduction so that their members share in the gains.

It is a very naive form of socialism that criticises technical change under the pretext that it causes unemployment. The real criticism that can be levied at capitalist economies in this regard is that they are too slow to adopt labour saving devices because labour is artificially cheap.

A good example of this could be seen in the computer industry. In the 1950s IBM developed highly automated machinery to construct the core memories for their computers. As demand grew their factories became more and more automatic. In 1965 they even had to open an entire new production line just to make the machines that would make the computers. Still they could not keep up with demand.

> The situation was becoming desperate. Then a newly appointed manger at Kingston who had spent several years in Japan, proposed that workers in the Orient could be found with sufficient manual dexterity and patience to wire core planes by hand.

Taking bags of cores, rolls of wire, and core frames to Japan, he returned ten days later with hand wired core planes as good as those that had been wired by automatic wire feeders at the Kingston plant. It was slow and tedious work but the cost of labor in the Orient was so low that production costs were actually lower than with full automation in Kingston. *See Pugh 1991, p209*

But in this respect the USSR was even worse.

The USSR subsidised food, rent, children's clothes and other necessities. The subsidy on basic goods compensated for low money wages. But subsidies, and social services had to be paid for out of the profits of nationalised industries (which formerly met most of the Soviet budget). For these to make a profit, wages had to be kept low, and low wages meant that the subsidies had to be retained!

The worst aspect of all this was that enterprises were encouraged by the cheapness of labour to be profligate with it. Why introduce modern automated machinery if labour was so cheap? Besides, it created work and prevented unemployment: real voodoo economics. True enough, any socialism worthy of the name must prevent unemployment, but that is not the same as creating unnecessary work. Its better to automate as fast as possible whilst reducing the working week.

Elaboration 1.4. *Nationalised ownership of industry held back international economic cooperation in comparison to the capitalist world.*

Modern capitalist industry is dominated by big multinational firms. Only these have the resources and size of market to reap economies of scale and meet the heavy research costs demanded by competition. The nationalised enterprises of Eastern Europe and to a lesser extent the USSR were just too small to gain such benefits.

2 Is planning still possible?

> Marxist economic theory, in conjunction with information technology provide the basis on which a viable socialist economic program can be advanced.

This is obviously a complex case to make out, and we can only give a few key points here.

Proposition 2.1. *Using modern computers it is possible to efficiently plan an economy in terms of natural units without recourse to the intermediary of money or markets.*

Ever since the 1920's bourgeois economists had been claiming that the problems of economic calculation involved with planing an economy were so complex that they could not be done. It was claimed that without the feedback mechanisms of the market decision making would be arbitrary and inefficient.

Whilst the Soviet economy had a rate of growth well in excess of the west these ideas did not seem very plausible. But when that its economy became more complex, and growth slowed, these criticisms seemed to gain relevance. It did seem plausible that a central planning agency could no longer cope with the myriad detail of a modern economy.

Elaboration 2.1. *Computerised input/output processing is the technique for detailed plan preparation.*

For the last decade or so we have been researching the possibilities of using modern computers to solve planning problems. We believe that it can now be conclusively demonstrated that the liberal arguments against socialist planning are outdated.[1] The problems of calculation that seemed daunting in the past can now be readily handled by super-computers.

If you think of a capitalist country one of the biggest users of computers is the financial sector. We have all seen TV footage of the money dealing rooms in the City banks where each desk seems to be crammed with a number of screens that is positively indecent. In contrast, main economic use of computers under socialism should be the simulation of detailed plans. In the USSR, the planning authority GOSPLAN was for some years a heavy user of mainframe computers.

In theory since GOSPLAN controled all of industry, it should have been able to exactly balance the needs and requirements of different industries. If it knew how many personal computers and how many mainframes it had ordered the computer manufactures to produce it would know exactly how many memory chips were going to be needed for that. It could order the semiconductor factories to turn out just that number of chips to the right specification. Theoretically this should be better than the situation in the West where the separate plans of computer and chip manufactures lead to periodic 'memory chip droughts'.

The theory seemed born out up until the about the mid 60's. Up until then the Russians out-performed the West in terms of economic growth.

---

[1] For a longer presentation of the argument see Cockshott 1990, Cottrell 1989.

Then the scale of the economy just got too big for the planners to handle. There were too many different products to keep track of. It was beyond the capability of a human bureaucracy to to balance the plans. Shortages of some products were combined with overproduction of others.

In the '60s economic cyberneticians had pointed out that the mathematical requirements for planning an economy were well understood. If it was beyond human capability you just needed to program computers to do it.

The results of trying to do this were disappointing. Of course it was not just in the USSR that the benefits of computerisation were greatly oversold in the '60s. Over here too, people attempted things that were really way beyond the rather limited abilities of the computers then available but since then the growth in computer speed has been astronomical. A modern supercomputer is about 100,000 times faster than its 1960's counterpart. Many people are now familiar with the spreadsheet programs like Excel that are used on personal computers to prepare company plans. The problem of drawing up a plan for an economy can be thought of as a giant spreadsheet or matrix.

The rows of the the spreadsheet represent the different economic activities, the columns represent the products used by these activities. If the first row represented electricity production and the second represented oil production then [row 1, col 2] would be the amount of oil used to produce electricity and [row 2, col 1] the amount of electricity used to produce oil.

The last column of the spreadsheet will hold the total amount produced by each process, so many tera-kilowatt hours of electricity and so many hundred million barrels of oil etc. The bottom row of the spreadsheet shows the total inputs of each product used in all the production processes.

The problem is to ensure that the total output of each product is not less than the total use of that product.

What you know to start off with are the technical properties of the processes, one barrel of oil produces so many kilowatt hours. You also know what your stock of capital goods and means of production are at the start of the year. What you must do is allocate these to different production processes in such a way as to meet the above constraint.

The standard approach to this is to treat it as a linear programming problem and solve it using the simplex method(see Bland). The problem with this is the running time of an algorithm based on the simplex method will grow with the cube of the number of industries considered. Suppose there were 10 million distinct products made in a continental economy. Then you are talking of some 10^{21} computer instructions to solve the problem. This is too big even for the fastest computer.

What Soviet economic planners resorted to was running smaller spreadsheets. They handled only a few thousand key products and ran these through their mainframe computers as linear programs. For these the equations can be solved. This explains one of the strengths of the Russian economy. It did well on certain key projects like the space program which can be given priority in the planning process. But there just is not the computer power available to apply the same techniques more widely.

Elaboration 2.2. *When faced with an intractable problem in computation there are two approaches: throw more computer power at it or devise a more efficient program.*

The problem of economic planning is so complex that both approaches are necessary. The best that could be hoped for is a program whose running time rises in direct proportion to the size of the problem.

In planning terms this would mean a computer program whose running time was proportional to the number of products rather than the cube of the number of products. But when the number of products is up around 10 million you need a hugely powerful machine just to store the initial data, let alone perform the computation.

There do exist algorithms that have the desired properties we discuss them in Cocshott and Cottrell 1993. On the sorts of supercomputers now available, one would be talking of computer programs that would take a few hours to run. This is modest compared to what physicists do with computers.

There is no technical reason why any continental sized economy now could not have a completely planned system. Each work place would have PCs linked to a network of computers within the enterprise which would in turn be linked to a Continent wide network of supercomputers. The work place would build up a local spreadsheet of its production capabilities and raw materials requirements. These would be transmitted through the hierarchy of machines which would balance up supplies and demands and draw up plans accordingly. Effective central planning requires the following basic elements:

1. A system for arriving at (and periodically revising) a set of targets for final outputs, which incorporates information on both consumers' preferences and the relative cost of producing alternative goods (the appropriate metric for cost being left open for the moment).

2. A method of calculating the implications of any given set of final outputs for the the required gross outputs of each product. At this stage

there must also be a means of checking the feasibility of the resulting set of gross output targets, in the light of the constraints posed by labour supply and existing stocks of fixed means of production, before these targets are forwarded to the units of production.

The provision of these elements involves a number of preconditions, notably an adequate system for gathering and processing dispersed economic information and a rational metric for cost of production. We should also note at once the important and entirely valid point stressed by Nove (1977 and 1983): for effective central planning, it is necessary that the planners are able to carry out the above sorts of calculations in full disaggregated detail. In the absence of horizontal market links between enterprises, management at the enterprise level *"cannot* know what it is that society needs unless the centre informs it" (Nove, 1977: 86).[2] Thus if the centre is unable to specify a coherent plan in sufficient detail, the fact that the plan may be 'balanced' in aggregate terms is of little avail. Even with the best will in the world on the part of all concerned, there is no guarantee that the specific output decisions made at the enterprise level will mesh properly.This general point is confirmed by Yun (1988: 55), who states that as of the mid-1980s Gosplan was able to draw up material balances for only 2,000 goods in its annual plans. When the calculations of Gossnab and the industrial ministries are included, the number of products tracked rises to around 200,000, still far short of the 24 million items produced in the Soviet economy at the time. This discrepancy meant that it was "possible for enterprises to fulfill their plans as regards the nomenclature of items they have been directed to produce, failing at the same time to create products immediately needed by specific users".

Our argument below involves grasping this particular nettle: while we agree that "in a basically non-market model the centre must discover what needs doing" (Nove, 1977: 86), and we accept Yun's account of the failure of Gosplan to do so, we dispute Nove's contention that "the centre cannot do this in micro detail" (*ibid.*). Planners, he asserts, are forced to work in terms of aggregates. They can only specify general targets like 'we need 500 million screws', but they fail to say how many 5mm screws, 10mm screws etc, are needed. As a result the wrong mix of screws gets produced.

What would have been an impossibly complex problem to solve by

---

[2] With one reservation. If, say, the central plan calls for enterprise A to supply intermediate good x to enterprise B, where it will be used in the production of some further good y, and if the planners apprise A and B of this fact, is there not scope for 'horizontal' discussion between the two enterprises over the precise design specification of x? (That is, even in the absence of market relations between A and B.)

the old bureaucratic means, has become an eminently practical proposition using modern information technology. Such a computerised planning system could respond to events far faster than any market could hope to do, thus undermining the main objection raised by bourgeois economists as to the unwieldy nature of socialist planning.

Proposition 2.2. *Socialism requires the abolition of money and its replacement by a system of remuneration based on labour time. This is the key to promoting both equity and technological advance.*

It is clear both from a reading of Marx's own work, and from the whole tenor of 19th century socialism, that it was a common assumption that socialism would involve the abolition of money and the introduction of a system of payment based on labour vouchers.

> ..., the individual producer receives back from society - after the deductions have been made - exactly what he gives to it. What he has given to it is his individual quantum of labour. For example, the social working day consists of the sum of the individual hours of work; the individual labour time of the individual producer is the part of the social working day contributed by him, his share in it. He receives a certificate from society that he has furnished such and such a an amount of labour (after deducting his labour for the common funds), and with this certificate he draws from the social stock of consumption as much as the same amount of labour costs. The same amount of labour which he has given to society in one form he receives back in another. *See Marx 1875*

Marx qualified this as being only a first step towards greater equality, but it is far more radically egalitarian than anything achieved by hitherto existing socialism. The principle of payment in labour time recognizes only two sources of inequality in income: that some people may work longer than others, or, in a piece work system, some may work faster. It eliminates all other income inequalities based upon class, race, sex, grade or professional qualification.

Also, by forcing workplaces to pay workers the the full value created by their labour, it eliminates the squandering of labour brought about by low pay, and encourages the introduction of labour saving innovation. It provides, moreover, a rational and scientifically well founded basis for economic calculation. If goods are labelled with the labour required to make them, the arbitrary and irrational character of the old Soviet price system is avoided.

Number of products	Multiplications	Time taken in seconds: Uniprocessor	Multiprocessor
1,000	1,000,000,000	10	0.1
100,000	10^{15}	10^7	100,000
10,000,000	10^{21}	10^{13}	10^{11}

Tab. 1: Gaussian solution to labour values

Proposition 2.3. *It is theoretically and technically possible to compute labour values to within the degree of accuracy required for practical purposes.*

The proposals above rest on the assumption that it is possible to calculate the labour content of each product in the economy. The problem is in principle solvable since one has n unknown labour values related by a set of n linear production functions. The difficulty is not one of principle but of scale. When the number of products gets up into the millions, the calculation involved is nontrivial.

If we were to represent the problem in classic matrix terms, with an n by $(n+1)$ matrix, where the rows represent products and the columns represent produced inputs plus direct labour, analytic solution of the equations using Gaussian elimination gives a problem requiring n^3 multiplication operations and a slightly larger number of additions and subtractions. Table1 gives the computer requirements for this calculation assuming differing sizes of economy. We assume that the uniprocessor is capable of 10^8 multiplications a second, and that the multiprocessor can perform 10^{10} multiplications per second.

It can be seen that, taking compute time alone into account, even the multiprocessor would take 10^1 seconds, or over three thousand years, to produce a solution for an economy of 10 million products. As if this were not enough, the situation would be further complicated by the memory required to store the matrix, which grows as n^2. Since the largest currently feasible memories are of the order of 10^{10} words, this would set a limit on the size of problem that could be handled at about 100,000 products.

If, however, we take into account the sparseness of the matrix (i.e. the high proportion of zero entries, when it is specified in full detail) the problem becomes more tractable. Let us suppose that the number of different types of components that enter directly into the production of any single product is n^k where $0 < k < 1$. If we assume a value of 0.4 for k, which seems fairly conservative,[3] we find that memory requirements now grow

---
[3] This means, for instance, that in a 10 million product economy each product is assumed to have on average 631 direct inputs.

Number of products	Multiplications	Words of memory	Time taken in seconds: Uniprocessor	Multiprocessor
1,000	158,489	31,698	1.6×10^{-3}	1.6×10^{-5}
100,000	100,000,000	20,000,000	1	0.01
10,000,000	6.3×10^{10}	1.2×10^{10}	630	6.3

Tab. 2: Iterative solution to labour values (Assuming A=10)

as $n^{(1+k)} = n^{1.4}$. If we can further simplify the problem by using iterative numerical techniques (Gauss–Seidel or Jacobi) to obtain approximate solutions, we obtain a computational complexity function of order $An^{1.4}$, where A is a small constant determined by the accuracy required of the answer.

This reduces the problem to one that is clearly within the scope of current computer technology, as shown in Table 2. The most testing requirement remains the memory, but it is within the range of currently available machines.

From this we conclude that the computation of labour values is eminently feasible.

Proposition 2.4. *Consumer goods prices should be set at market clearing levels and the discrepancies between these prices and the values of goods used to determine the optimal levels of production.*

Given that supplies of and demand for goods is never exactly equal, it is only average prices that should equal labour values. Individual items in short supply would sell at a premium, balanced by those in oversupply selling at a discount. These premiums and discounts can them guide the planning authorities to decide which goods to produce more of, and which to produce less off.

Note that this does not in anyway presuppose the existence of private trade. Our proposal on this count might be described as 'Lange plus Strumilin'. From Lange we take up a modified version of the 'trial and error' process, whereby market prices for consumer goods are used to guide the re-allocation of social labour among the various consumer goods; from Strumilin we take the idea that in socialist equilibrium the use-value created in each line of production should be in a common proportion to the social labour time expended.[4] The central idea is this: the plan calls for

---
[4] This point—a basic theme of Strumilin's work over half a century—is expressed particularly clearly in his (1977: 136–7).

production of some specific vector of final consumer goods, and these goods are marked with their social labour content. If planned supplies and consumer demands for the individual goods happen to coincide when the goods are priced in accordance with their labour values, the system is already in equilibrium. In a dynamic economy, however, this is unlikely. If supplies and demands are unequal, the 'marketing authority' for consumer goods is charged with adjusting prices, with the aim of achieving (approximate) short-run balance, i.e.prices of goods in short supply are raised while prices are lowered in the case of surpluses.[5] In the next step of the process, the planners examine the ratios of market-clearing price to labour value across the various consumer goods. (Note that both of these magnitudes are denominated in labour-hours; labour content in the one case, and labour tokens in the other). Following Strumilin's conception, these ratios should be equal (and equal to unity) in long-run equilibrium. The consumer goods plan for the next period should therefore call for expanded output of those goods with an above-average price/value ratio, and reduced output for those with a below-average ratio.[6]

In each period, the plan should be balanced, using either input–output methods or an alternative balancing algorithm.[7] That is, the gross outputs needed to support the target vector of final outputs should be calculated in advance. This is in contrast to Lange's (1938) system, in which the very coherence of the plan—and not only its optimality—seems to be left to 'trial and error'. Our scheme, however, does not impose the unreasonable requirement that the pattern of consumer demand be perfectly anticipated *ex ante*; adjustment in this respect is left to an iterative process which takes place in historical time.[8]

This scheme meets the objection of Nove (1983), who argues that labour values cannot provide a basis for planning even if they gave a valid measure of cost of production. Nove's point is that labour content of itself tells us nothing about the use-value of different goods. Of course this is true,[9]

---

[5] With market-clearing prices, of course, the goods go to those willing to pay the most. Given an egalitarian distribution of income, we see no objection to this.

[6] Naturally, an element of demand forecasting is also called for here: the current ratios provide a useful guide rather than a completely mechanical rule.

[7] An alternative algorithm which makes allowance for given stocks of specific means of production is given in Cockshott (1990).

[8] In his later reflection on the socialist calculation debate, Lange (1967) seems to suggest that an optimal plan can be pre-calculated by computer, without the need for the real-time trial and error he envisaged in 1938. Insofar as this would require that consumer demand functions are all known in advance, this seems to us far-fetched.

[9] As was clearly understood by Marx: "On a given basis of labour productivity the production of a certain quantity of articles in every particular sphere of production re-

but it only means that we need an independent measure of consumers' valuations; and the price, in labour tokens, which roughly balances planned supply and consumer demand provides just such a measure. By the same token, we can answer a point made by Mises in his discussion of the problems faced by socialism under dynamic conditions (1951: 196ff). One of the dynamic factors he considers is change in consumer demand, à propos of which he writes: "If economic calculation and therewith even an approximate ascertainment of the costs of production were possible, then within the limits of the total consumption-units assigned to him, each individual citizen could be allowed to demand what he liked...." But, he continues, "since, under socialism, no such calculations are possible, all such questions of demand must necessarily be left to the government". Our proposal allows for precisely the consumer choice that Mises claims is unavailable.

Proposition 2.5. *The funding of the surplus product should come from taxes on income, approved by referendum.*

In any society a certain proportion of the social product must be set aside for investment and to support those unable to work etc. In a socialism based on labour values, this would be expressed as a deduction of so many hours work a week that had to be performed for the community. If the phrase had not been purloined, one might call it the community charge.

In the countries of hitherto existing socialism the decision as to how the social working day was to be divided between necessary and surplus labour time was taken by the government. As, over time, the government became alienated from the working classes, the process became exploitative. The state as an alien power was depriving the workers of the fruits of their labour.

To prevent this, it is essential, that the division of the working day between social and necessary labour, be decided by the working class itself; rather than by a government which claims to act in its interests. There should be an annual vote by the working population to decide on the level of the tax. A multiple choice ballot could allow the people to decide between more public services or more consumption.

Only when the surplus product is provided voluntarily does it cease to be exploitation.

---

quires a definite quantity of social labour-time; although this proportion varies in different spheres of production and has no inner relation to the usefulness of these articles or the special nature of their use-values." (1972: 186-7)

Incentives

One worry that people may have about the Marxian proposal for socialism is that it would remove all incentives, but this is probably a misunderstanding. Payment for labour does not necessarily mean everyone earns the same. The stakanovite system in Russia was based on payment according to labour and was explicitly introduced to give workers a greater incentive to produce higher output. In it the intensity of labour was measured by the volume of output. If you have a set of individuals doing the same task, then you can validly measure the work done by the output produced.

But where the work is of different types then such output comparisons are not possible. It is possible, when work is of different kinds, to measure the calories expended, so that somebody doing hard labouring who expends a lot of calories can be objectively said to work harder than somebody in a sedentary job. The Soviet payment system took this into account so that oil workers and miners got paid extra for the heavy labour that they did. But when this issue is raised in the West, what the critic is likely to mean is the distinction between mental and manual labour. The prejudice of our society is, that since doctors for example, have to train for 6 years to qualify, they should be paid more to give people an incentive to be doctors. The cultural relativity of this concept is born out by the fact that the USSR had no shortage of doctors, even though doctors were paid less than coal miners. Surgeons did not flock from hospitals to go down the mines.

One must be careful to distinguish rent incomes from necessary incentives. If an education system, whether through inadequate funding, class barriers to entry etc, fails to produce enough doctors, then doctors can command a rent income. If the education system, as part of comprehensive national labour-power planning, turns out large numbers of doctors, and if this education is free to the students, then there will be no shortage of doctors. As Neurath pointed out, the status and health risks of an occupation must be taken into account when assessing the rewards it brings.

A possibly more serious objection relates to incentives for managers. What incentive would they have to act in the social rather than their private interest?

If one assumed that socialist industry was going to be managed by an extension of the civil service bureaucracy then it is evident that different societies at different times have more or less efficient and honest bureaucracies. Neurath was writing in the context of his experience with the notoriously efficient German civil service in the Great War. The question of what historical conditions allow an honest and efficient bureaucracy to exist is an interesting one, but not one we would claim to have special answers for. But it is clear, that the less the temptations to personal financial enrichment, the greater will be the prospects for honesty. In this context, a non-monetary economy starts out with considerable safeguards against corruption.

But one does not have to assume that a socialist industry would be managed by a civil service hierarchy. There is a long tradition of socialist writers[10] warning that although a socialist bureaucracy may not be personally venal, in the way the Russian bureacracy became after the fall of communism, it can be collectively venal. It can act to further its social interest as a group at the expense of the rest of society.

An alternative is for management groups to be elected by or selected from among the workers they manage. In this case the relevant model of incentives are those which apply to elected politicians - the incentive to please their electorate, and the problem becomes how does one align the interests of the production collective with society as a whole. The starting point for this has to be the observation that people become attached to the group that they work with, whether these be those working in a public institution, a regiment or a division of a firm. If a socialist economy operates an accounting model in which the labour budget allocated to a project or division depends upon the final consumption of its product (regulated by a consumer goods market as described above), then this collective loyalty can be brought into play. Since people will not want their team reduced, or even broken up, the collectivity has an incentive to work towards producing goods that society wants[11]. If a project is making goods that nobody wants, the planning system will scale back production and each individual stands either to loose friends, or at worst be redeployed somewhere else. Thus the team as a whole has an incentive to work for the social good.

Industrial and social democracy are the key factors here.

3 Democracy Planning and the Internet

> The socialist movement has never developed a correct constitutional program. In particular it has accepted the misconception that elections are a democratic form.

---

[10] One thinks of Trotsky (2004), Djilas (1957), and even Stalin if Furr (2005) is to be believed.

[11] For a discussion of the formal role assigned to such collective in the late Soviet System see the Lavignes (1979).

The same electronic technology that makes planning feasible enables direct democratic control over the planning process. It is now quite feasible to provide every household with an Internet terminal[12] that people could use to vote on what sort of plans they want.

Using the wealth of up to date economic data that the planning networks gathered, together with the power of super-computers, rival political parties could simulate different continental plans. Each would provide full employment but bbe directed towards different ends: improving public transport, investing more in industry, implementing energy saving measures, improving housing conditions, etc. These could be debated on TV and in the media. On-line databases would allow citizens to query the implications of the different plans.

People could then use their Internet terminals to vote for which of these development plans they wanted; knowing that the various alternatives had been thoroughly costed and proved feasible.

Proposition 3.1. *Soviets and elections on universal suffrage are both ultimately aristocratic forms of government.*

Aristocracy means rule by the best.

In a feudal society, landowners are self evidently the best, most honorable, most noble elements of society. But this does not limit aristocracy as a principle to feudalism. Aristocracy simply means an elitist system of government.

Aristotle argued that any political system based upon elections was an aristocracy. (*See Aristotle pp 286*). It introduces the deliberate element of choice, of selection of the best, the *aristoi*, in place of government by all of the people. What he implies, as would be evident to any Marxist, is that the 'best' people in a class society will be the better off. The poor, the scum and the riff-raff are of course 'unsuitable' candidates for election. Wealth and respectability go together.

In a bourgeois parliamentary system this *aristoi* is comprised in the main of men of high social status: lawyers, business men etc. In a soviet system the *aristoi* who get elected onto the local soviets, and still more those who get promoted from the local to the supreme soviets, are initially the elite of the working class. They are the politically active, the class conscious, the self-confident, in short, activists of the Communist Party.

The leading role of the Communist Party, translates it, in an electoral mechanism with a purely proletarian constituency, into the aristocracy of

---

[12] Limited capability Internet terminals can be cheaply built into TV sets.

labour. As such it becomes prey to the characteristic corruptions of aristocracy. Soviets, based as they are on the electoral principle, transform themselves from instruments of proletarian democracy into their opposite.

This degeneration is not accidental, not to be explained away by historical contingencies, but inevitable .

Elaboration 3.1. *Democracy is an ancient term for a type of popular rule based upon mass assemblies and selection of officials by lot. What has come to be termed democracy in the 20th century has almost nothing in common with this original meaning.*

The political systems that currently label themselves democracies are all oligarchies. The fact that they can still get away with calling themselves democracies is one of the most remarkable confidence tricks in history. (*See Finlay 1985*).

In his dsytopian novel '1984' Orwell makes ironic reference to Newspeak, a dialect of English so corrupted that phrases like 'freedom is slavery' or 'war is peace' could pass unremarked. What he was alluding to is the power of language to control our thoughts. When those in authority can redefine the meanings of words they make subversion literally unthinkable. The phrase 'parliamentary democracy' is an example of newspeak: a contradiction in disguise. Go back to the Greek origins of the word democracy. The second half of the word means 'power' or 'rule'. Hence we have autocracy ; rule by one man; aristocracy, rule by the aristoi the best people, the elite; democracy meant rule by the demos. Most comentators translate this a rule by the people, but the word demos had a more specific meaning. It meant rule by the common people or rule by the poor. Aristotle, describing the democracies of his day was quite explicit about the fact that democracy meant rule by the poor. Countering the argument that democracies simply meant rule by the majority he gave the following example:

> Suppose a total of 1,300; 1000 of these are rich, and they give no share in office to the 300 poor, who are also free men and in other respects like them; no one would say that these 1300 lived under a democracy

(Politics 1290).

But he says this is an artificial case, "**due to the fact that the rich are everywhere few, and the poor numerous.**" As a specific definition he gives:

> A democracy exists whenever those who are free and are not well off, being in a majority, are in sovereign control of the gov-

ernment, an oligarchy when control lies in the hands of the rich and better born, these being few.

In the original meanings of the words what exists even in countries that are termed parliamentary democracies is oligarchy not democracy. In its origins,'democracy' meant rule by the working poor. In modern language : workers power or proletarian rule (the proles being the latin equivalent of the greek demos). We can see how far a parliamentary system is from a democracy in practice by looking at the actual institutions of the *demokratia*

The first and most characteristic feature of *demokratia* was rule by the majority vote of all citizens. This was generally by a show of hands at a sovereign assembly or *eklesia*. The sovereignty of the *demos* was not delegated to an elected chamber of professional politicians as in the bourgeois system. Instead the ordinary working people, in those days the peasantry and traders, gathered together en masse to discuss, debate and vote on the issues concerning them. The similarity between the *eklesia* and those spontaneous organisations of modern workers democracy: the mass strike meetings that are so hated by the bourgeois world, is immediately apparent.

The second important institution were the peoples law courts or *dikasteria*. These courts had no judges, instead the dicasts acted as both judge and jury. The dicasts were chosen by lot from the citizen body, using a sophisticated procedure of voters tickets and allotment machines, and once in court decisions were taken by ballot and could not be appealed against. It was regarded by Aristotle that control of the courts gave the *demos* control of the constitution.

There was no government as such, instead the day to day running of the state was entrusted to a council of officials drawn by lot. The council had no legislative powers and was responsible merely for enacting the policies decided upon by the people.

Participation in the state was restricted to citizens. This excluded women, slaves and *metics* or in modern terms resident aliens.

Only where skill was essential, as with military commanders, was election considered safe. The contrast with our political and military system could not be more striking.

A neo-classical democracy would still be a state in the Marxian sense. It would be an organised public power, to which minorities are forced to submit. The *demos* would use it to defend their rights against any remaining or nascent exploiting class. But it would be acephalous: a state without a head of state, without the hierarchy that marks a state based on class exploitation.

The various organs of public authority would be controlled by citizens' committees chosen by lot. The media, the health service, the planning and marketing agencies, the various industries would have their juries. Each of these would have a defined area of competence. A committee for the energy industry, for instance, would decide certain details of energy policy but it could not disregard a popular vote, say, to phase out nuclear power. The membership of the committees need not be uniformly drawn from the public. The health service committees could be made up partly of a random sample of health service workers, and partly of members of the public. As Burnheim argues, the principle should be that all those who have a legitimate interest in the matter should have a chance to participate in its management.

This view is radically different from both Social Democracy and the practice of hitherto-existing socialism. Planning, for example, is not under government control but under a supervisory committee of ordinary citizens, who, since they are drawn by lot, will be predominantly working people. In the sense that they are autonomous of any government, these committees can be thought of as analogous to the autonomous bodies of bourgeois civil society: independent central banks, broadcasting authorities, arts councils, research councils etc. It is not necessary for them to be under direct state control; their charters and the social backgrounds of their governors ensure their function. Provided that the socialist analogues of such authorities have founding charters open to popular amendment, that they have supervisory committees who are socially representative of the people, and that their deliberations are public, popular control would be assured.

The powers of demarchic councils would be either regulatory or economic or both. An advanced industrial society requires a complex body of regulations to function. In present society some of these regulations are what we recognise as laws, emanating from the decisions of politicians and enforced by state power, but a larger part already originate in autonomous bodies. Professional organisations define codes of practice binding on their members. Trade organisations define standards for industrial components, something absolutely essential for rapid technological progress. International bodies define standards for the exchange of electronic data by telephone, telegraph and fax.

In many cases these regulations affect only the internal operation of particular branches of production or social activity, and the composition of their regulating councils should remain limited to people who participate in that area. In others—areas like broadcasting or processes which may impinge upon public health—general social interests are affected. In these cases the regulating council would have to be extended to include a majority of other citizens, selected by lot to represent the public interest,

The other powers of demarchic councils would stem from their command over resources, human or inanimate. A council might be entrusted with the administration of certain immobile public property: buildings, historic monuments, transport routes, energy and water supply facilities. To the extent that these are immobile, the principal contradictions that may arise are over access. One thinks here of how the propertarian-dominated British commission responsible for ancient monuments denied the dispossessed access to Stonehenge. But to the extent that the property deteriorates and has to be maintained, even immobile properties presuppose an influx of labour and materials.

A council will also be entrusted with mobile public property in the form of machinery, vehicles and raw materials. This is more significant for demarchies administering manufacturing processes, but would affect them all to some extent. We assume that all such mobile property is ultimately allocated by the national plan. A council running a project has the use of the property unless and until a more urgent use arises.

Finally a council disposes of the labour of the members of its project. Since this labour is a fraction of society's total labour, and could potentially be devoted to other activities, it is, from the standpoint of the national accounts, abstract social labour. Similarly, the flow of mobile public property into the project presupposes a fraction of society's labour being devoted to the reproduction of these items. As a flow, therefore, it too is abstract social labour. The dynamic economic power of a council is, finally, command over social labour.

The magnitude of its power is measured in the hours of its labour budget. But by what right does it gain this power and who regulates its magnitude?

It is a power that is either devolved or in the last resort delegated by the people themselves. Consider a council administering a school. Its power might be devolved from some local or national educational council who vote it an annual labour budget. Let us assume that schooling is a local matter. In that case, the budget of the local education council would be set by the local electorate who would annually decide how many hours were to be deducted from their year's pay to fund education.

In the case of a manufacturing council, the delegation is more indirect. Its products—perhaps lead-acid storage batteries—meet an indirect social rather than concrete and local need. The number of batteries that society needs is a function of how many cars, telephone exchanges, portable radios, etc. are manufactured. Only the national, or in the long term federal, planning authority can calculate this. Thus only the planning authority can delegate a budget for battery production.

In all cases the people are the ultimate delegators of power. Either they vote to tax themselves and entrust a demarchic council with a budget to produce a free service, or they choose to purchase goods, in which case they are voting labour time to the production of those goods.

The great virtue of the rule of the *demos* was the elaborate constitutional mechanism they evolved to defend their power against usurpation by the upper classes. That rule flourished for some two centuries until crushed by the Macedonian and Roman empires. During that period it generated a beacon of art, architecture, philosophy, science and culture that illuminated the subsequent dark centuries. The Enlightenment golden age of bourgeois culture was a self conscious reflection of that light. The torch will not truly be reignited till the modern *demos* come to power.

4 The criticisms of the Austrian school

The best known criticisms of the possibility of a rational socialist economy come from the Austrian school whose most prominent representatives were Mises and Hayek. There is an extensive literature on their criticisms of socialism but in the context of this article we intend to concentrate on a limited number of points:

1. The possibility of economic calculation *in-natura*. The proposal for in-natura calculation stems from Neurath (1919), and was criticised by Mises. We will argue below that it is not only possible but is becoming increasingly relevant in light of the Kyoto protocol.

2. The possibility of using labour as a unit of account criticised by both Neurath and Mises. This was dealt with above, but we will say a bit more below.

3. The criticism of Hayek relating to information flows in socialist economies. This centers around the notion of the price system as a telecoms network which conveys key information to regulate a market economy, and the assertion that because of tacit knowledge held by agents, a non market system of regulation would fail.

In his 1919 paper, Neurath argues that the experience of the German war economy allowed one to see certain key weaknesses of past economic thought.

> Conventional economic theory mostly stands in too rigid a connection to monetary economics and has until now almost entirely neglected the in-kind economy.(Neurath 1919, p 300)

The war economy had in contrast been largely an in-kind economy.

> As a result of the war the in-kind calculus was applied more often and more systematically than before... It was all to apparent that war was fought with ammunition and the supply of food, not with money.(Neurath 1919, p304)

Neuraths emphasis on in-kind statistics related both to conditions of life of the population and to the internal regulation of an administrative economy. If one wanted to know whether real quality of life of the population was improving or not one had to examine their lives in material not money terms.

Compared to such statistics in kind, figures for national income were, he said, far less revealing. In particular he cautions against accepting the notion of 'real income' or inflation adjusted money income as a surrogate for the quality of life.

> The current concept of consumption, [so-called] real income, is also understandable as derivative of money calculation. Given our own approach to economic efficiency, it seems appropriate to comprehend also :work and illness under the concept which covers food, clothing, housing, theatre visits, etc. These things, however, are not part of the [current] concept of consumption and real income, which covers only what appears as a reflection of money income. ...Occupational prestige, for example, is as much a part of one's income as eating and drinking. (Neurath 1917, page 336)

What Neurath was saying here looks very modern. It is notable that this aspect of Neurath's argument for in-kind economics has been neglected by von Mises or his followers. Indeed Neurath argues that von Mises himself ultimately has recourse to the notion of an in-kind substratum of welfare against which different monetary measures of welfare must be judged. Mises recognises that monopoly reduces welfare thus:

> The difference between the values of these goods and the higher value of the quantity of monopoly goods not produced represents the loss in welfare which the monopoly has inflicted on the national economy." If, in the case of monopoly, according to

Mises, there is a calculation of wealth by which one can judge money calculation, then it should always be available and allow judgment on all economic processes. (Neurath Economic Writings, page 429)

Neurath was adamant that a socialist economy had to be moneyless because of:

1. The non-comensurability of final outcomes in terms not only of quality of life, but the quality of life of future generations. This follows from his emphasis on non-commodity factors in the quality of social life.

2. The complexity of the technical constraints on production.

The emphasis on non-comensurability has its roots in his ideas on the measurement of outcomes, quality of life now and quality of life in the future:

> Savings in coal, trees, etc., beyond amounting to savings in the displeasure of work, mean the preservation of future pleasure, a positive quantity. Saving certain raw materials can become pointless if one discovers something new. The freezing people of the future only show up if there is already now a demand for future coal.(Economic Writings, page 470)

Like von Mises he argues that labour time calculations are inadequate for the internal regulation of production. Labour time calculations presuppose a long time frame and an absence of natural resource constraints. If there are natural resource constraints, or short term shortages of particular equipment they can misrepresent what is potentially producible.

> How can points be assigned to individual articles of consumption? If there were natural work units and if it could be determined how many natural work units, in a "socially necessary" way, have been spent on each article of consumption, and if further it were possible to produce any amount of each article, then, under some additional conditions, each article could be assigned the number of points that represent its "work effort". [...] If there is a great demand for articles made from these raw materials, either rationing will have to be introduced or the number of points for their distribution will have to be increased beyond the number representing the work spent on their production. Conversely articles in little demand will be offered for fewer points than would the work spent for their production. (Economic Writings, pp. 435-436)

4.1 In kind calculation and the Kyoto protocol

Neurath's concern with natural resource constraints is obviously relevant in today's world. In our proposals we allow for marked labour content and selling prices to diverge provided both are clearly marked on the product so that the consumer knows if they are getting good 'value for money'. If goods are marked up due to a temporary shortage of supply, the fact that the labour value of the good as well as its current selling price is displayed in the shops means that consumers can contrast the market price with what Smith called the 'natural price', and hold off consumption in the expectation that prices will fall.

This would not work in the case of abiding natural resource constraints. Suppose an administative economy has to abide by the Kyoto protocol. It then has two over-arching constraints on production – the available labour force and the allowed emissions of CO_2. If we allow the consumer goods market to move to an equilibrium where prices coincide with labour values, then we will have a particular vector of final outputs. Just as one can compute labour values one can in principle compute the 'carbon' value of any product or process - this is what Neurath's in-kind calculus implies.

We now have three vectors λ the vector of per-unit labour values, κ the vector of per-unit carbon values, and y the market clearing vector of final outputs when market prices equal labour values. In an economy not bound by the Kyoto protocol, the plan or market must meet the constraint $P \geq \lambda.y$ where P is the working population measured in full time persons[13], and . denotes inner product. Suppose that we have a Kyoto limit on carbon emissions of K then the economy must meet the constraint $K \geq \kappa.y'$ where y' is the actual output vector.

If y the market clearing vector for prices=values, is such that $K < \kappa.y$ then we have a problem. Either all output is proportionately scaled back such that

$$y' = y(\frac{K}{\kappa.y})$$

with a consequent under utilisation of labour resources, or the plan devises a set of re-scaling weights w such that $y' = (y \cdot w)$ with . being Hadamard product, such that both the full employment and Kyoto constraints are met. The market clearing price for y' will not necessarily guarantee that prices are still equal to labour values.

---

[13] Some dimensional analysis helps here. Labour values have dimension person-hours = persons×time. y has dimension unit of output per unit time, so $\lambda.y$ has dimension persons.

The end result will be that certain products, whose production ultimately produces large quantities of CO_2 will end up being sold above their labour values.

Unless and until one has carried out real calculations with real input output tables it is difficult to determine how large will be the induced deviation of prices from values resulting from abiding by the Kyoto protocol.

Suppose for example, that λ and κ turn out to be highly correlated, or in other words, the angles between the vectors are small. This would make it difficult to meet the Kyoto constraint whilst meeting the full employment target, since change in weights which reduce $y.\kappa$ will also reduce $y.\lambda$.

Suppose instead that λ and κ turn out to be weakly correlated, or in geometric terms, that the two vectors are at a substantial angle. In this case there will be a large number of rescalings w that will ensure both Kyoto and employment constraints are met. If the system has a sufficiently high number of degrees of freedom (broad classes of products), then it should be possible to exploit 'decoherence' to minimise the eventual deviations between prices and values. The point here is that CO_2 is produced directly or indirectly by almost every production process. A first order solution to meeting Kyoto would involve reducing the scale of those industries i with the highest values $\frac{\kappa_i}{\lambda_i}$, since these reduce carbon emissions fastest whilst causing the least unemployment.

Suppose that a 5% reduction in CO_2 emissions is being sought. Suppose that the use of oil for heating has a high $\frac{\kappa_i}{\lambda_i}$ whereas the growth of fruit has a much lower $\frac{\kappa_i}{\lambda_i}$. This implies that the planning authorities could scale back heating oil production and transfer oil workers to fruit packing plants and so help meet the Kyoto targets, whilst maintaining full employment. The effect on the market clearing prices for consumer goods would be that heating oil would rise above its labour value whilst fruit fell below its labour value, but since both industries are government owned, the notional losses incurred by fruit production could offset the notional 'profit' in fuel oil. Changes in price due to meeting the Kyoto protocol could then be marked as a 'green tax' or a 'green subsidy' on the final price of the goods.

But if the state wholesaling authorities had statistics on the elasticity of demand for different products, they could employ a more sophisticated rule.

Let e_i be the elasticity of demand of the ith product. Then the planners should preferentially scale back those industries for which $e_i \frac{\kappa_i}{\lambda_i}$ is highest and redeploy workers to industries for which $e_i \frac{\kappa_i}{\lambda_i}$ is lowest. The net effect is to allow both employment and Kyoto targets to be met with the minimal deviation of prices from labour values.

So Neurath was right about labour values being insufficient for the internal regulation of production. Instead he advocates detailed statistics on the consumption and use of each raw material and intermediate product - what would later be called an in-kind input output table. But as the example above, of meeting the Kyoto protocol shows, meeting such environmental constraints is much easier for a fully planned economy. An economy controlled by detailed in-kind calculations can readily determine if a particular mix of output will achieve a 5% cut in greenhouse gas emissions whilst meeting employment targets. Wholesale prices can later be adjusted to ensure consumer goods markets clear. In only price mechanisms are allowed as a control over greenhouse gas emissions governments face the problems that:

- They will probably not have the detailed in-kind statistics needed to tell upon which products or processes to levy carbon taxes.

- The response of aggregate demand to these price signals is uncertain, so if the performance of countries so far is anything to go on, the Kyoto targets are unlikely to be met until many iterations of adjusting green taxes have occured.

- If governments err in the other direction, by increasing green taxes very sharply to ensure meeting Kyoto targets, they are likely to depress employment.

4.2 Market or plan - which suffers information loss

At the time that Neurath and von Mises engaged in their initial debates (1920s) the algorithmic techniques required for detailed in-kind calculations had not been developed. The subsequent work of Remak, von Neumann and Kantorovich laid the mathematical basis for the type of calculations we illustrate above. Mises had argued in particular that in the absence of prices there was no practical method of selecting which of several production alternatives would be optimal. If we consider the matrix notation for the technical structure of the economy introduced by Remak (1929) and von Neumann (1945), we can understand why Neurath was so adamant that socialist calculation had to be performed in kind and could not be reduced to accounting in a single surrogate unit like labour or energy. When we do accounting in money, or in a surrogate like labour, then we add up the total cost of each column of the I/O matrix, giving us a vector of final output in money terms.

Suppose C is an $n \times n$ square matrix, and p an n dimensional vector. By applying Iverson's (1979) reshaping operator ρ, we can map C to a vector of length n^2 thus $\mathbf{c} \leftarrow (n \times n)\rho C$, and we thus see that the price system, having n dimensions involves a massive dimension reduction from the n^2 dimensional vector $\mathbf{c}$. If that is the case, then any calculations that can be done with the information in the reduced system p could in principle be done, by some other algorithmic procedure starting from C.

Remak(1929) showed for the first time how, starting from an *in-natura* description of the conditions of production, one can derive an equilibrium system of prices. This implies that the *in-natura* system contains the information necessary for the prices and that the prices are a projection of the *in-natura* system onto a lower dimensional space. *A price system thus represents an enormous destruction of information.* A matrix of technical coefficients is folded down to a vector, and in the process the real *in-natura* constraints on the economy are lost sight of. This destruction of information means that an economy that works only on the basis of the price vector must blunder around with only the most approximate grasp of reality. This of course, is exactly the opposite proposition to that advanced by Mises.

How then can such a reduced information structure function to regulate the economy?

How can it work if it allows "individual producers to watch merely the movement of a few pointers"[14]?

Prices do convey objective information about the social costs of production, through the noise of their fluctuations the signal of labour value shines through[15]. Because of this they may well function as a regulator of production. Divergences of prices above or below values could serve to attract or repel labour resources into and from branches of production. It is one thing to recognize that this is possible, another to assess its importance in regulating the economy. Posted prices are not the only telecoms system the economy has. Actual orders for commodities are another. Firms set prices and then get orders which are specified in quantities, and in qualities and times. An order or quote specifies fairly precisely in-kind what

---

[14] It is more than a metaphor to describe the price system as a kind of machinery for registering change, or a system of telecommunications which enables individual producers to watch merely the movement of a few pointers, as an engineer might watch the hands of a few dials, in order to adjust 5 their activities to changes of which they may never know more than is reflected in the price movements. (Hayek, 1945, p. 527)

[15] Those skeptical of this proposition should consult recent econometric studies of the matter, eg, Petrovic (1987), Ochoa (1989), Cockshott and Cottrell (1997), Shaikh (1998), Zachariah (2006).

is being ordered, and when it is to be delivered. If a business manager paid attention only to the prices she sold things at and ignored the quantities being ordered, the firm would not survive long. Apriori one can not say whether the price channel or the in-kind channel is more significant in regulating the economy. Far from being hidden and private, this in-kind information has to be disclosed between users and suppliers. The information has, moreover, an objective embodiment in a commercial correspondance which is increasingly electronic. These electronic in-kind flows of information, which already exist under capitalism, are what the internet could capture for a socialist plan.

We will leave aside for now the relative importance of the price and in-kind channels in economic information flows, and concentrate on how a single vector of prices might act as a contributory regulator for a complex matrix of inter-sector flows. There seem to be two basic reasons why it could work:

One is the universality of human labour which means that it is possible to associate with each commodity a single scalar number - price - which indirectly represents the amount of labour that was used to make it. Deviations of relative prices from relative values can then allow labour to move from where it is less socially necessary to where it is more necessary. But this is only possible because all economic activity comes down in the end to human activity. Were that not the case, a single indicator would not be sufficient to regulate the consumption of inputs that were fundamentally of different dimensions. It is only because the dimension of all inputs is ultimately labour - direct or indirect that prices can regulate activity.

Another answer lies in the computational tractability of systems of linear equations. Consider the method that we gave in Cottrell and Cockshott (1992) for computing the labour values of commodities from an input output table. We made an initial estimate of the value of each commodity and then used the I/O table to make successively more precise estimates. What we have here is an iterative functional system where we repeatedly apply a function to the value vector to arrive at a new value vector. Because the mapping is what is termed a contractive affine transform the functional system has an attractor to which it converges. For a discussion of such systems see Barnsley (1988), in particular Chapter 3.. This attractor is the system of labour values. The system must constitute a contractive transform because any viable economy must have a net surplus product in its basic sector. Hence an initial error in the estimate of the value of an input commodity is spread over a larger quantity of the commodity on output and thus after an iteration the percentage error must decline.

The process that we described algorithmically in Cottrell and Cockshott (1992) is what happens in a distributed manner in a real capitalist economy as prices are being formed. Firms add up wage costs and costs of other commodity inputs, add a mark-up and set their prices accordingly. This distributed algorithm, which is nowadays carried out by a combination of people and company computers, is structurally similar to that we described. It too, constitutes a contractive affine transform which converges on a price vector. The exact attractor is not relevant at this point, what is relevant is that the iterative functional system has a stable attractor. It has this because the process of economic production can be well approximated by a piecewise contractive linear transform on price or value space. Were it the case that production processes were strongly non linear such that the output of say corn were a polynomial, then the iterative functional system would be highly unstable, and the evolution of the entire price system would be completely chaotic and unpredictable. Prices would then be useless as a guide to economic activity[16].

Neither of the two factors above are specific to a market economy. Labour is the key universal resource in any society prior to full robotisation. By the full version of the Church-Turing thesis if a problem coud be solved by a distributed collection human computers, then it can be solved by a Universal Computer. If it is tractable for a distributed collection of humans it is also algorithmically tractable when calculated by the computers of a socialist planning agency. The very factors which make the price system relatively stable and useful are the factors which make socialist econonomic calculation tractable.

4.3 Advances since Mises

Remak formalised the derivation of prices from in-natura data, and expressed confidence that with the development of electric calculating machines, the required large systems of linear equations will be solvable in a socialist economy.

The weakness of Remak's analysis was that it was limited to an economy in steady state. Mises had acknowledged that socialist calculation would be possible under such circumstances.

Von Neumann took the debate on in two distinct ways:

1. He models an economy in growth, not a static economy. He assumes an economy in uniform proportionate growth. He explicitly abjures

---

[16] For the instability of such systems see Becker and Dorfler (1989) or Baker and Gollub (1990).

considering the effects of restricted natural resources or labour supply, assuming instead that the labour supply can be extended to accommodate growth. This is perhaps not unrealistic as a picture of an economy undergoing rapid industrialization (for instance Soviet Russia at the time he was writing). His description of the economy is so general that it could apply to either a market or an administrative economy.

2. He allows for there to be multiple techniques to produce any given good - Remak only allowed one. These different possible productive techniques use different mixtures of inputs, and only some of them will be viable.

What are the significant results here?

- The *in − natura* techniques available to the economy, which he captured in his use and produce matrices A, B determine which processes of production should be used and in which intensities.

- They also determine an equilibrium set of prices. No system of subjective preferences is required to derive these.

- The *in-natura* techniques also determine the rate of growth and rate of interest.

But although von Neuman showed the existence of an equilibrium growth path determined by in-kind constraints he neither showed how a capitalist economy would gravitate to this path, nor did provide specific algorithmic techniques by which a planning body could determine how to reach this path. In causal terms he shows that in-kind conditions determine which production techiques are viable, but it remains an open question whether this required calculations in prices (which his model also has).

This specific problem of the algorithmic procedure to derive an optimal plan was solved by Kantorovich (1960) when he invented the technique of linear optimisation. Linear optimisation allows a planning problem specified entirely in-kind to be optimally solved without recourse to the price mechanism Kantorovich's original technique of resolving multipliers is, in the western literature, refered to as the use of shadow prices. Kantorovich prefered the term Objective Valuations, since these were not prices at which goods were exchanged, but numbers used to guide an algorithmic process. Later interior point methods of solving linear optimisation dispense even with these resolving multipliers(Anderson and Gonzio 1996). Thus we can say that it has been definitely shown that, contra Mises, in kind optimisation, without prices, is both theoretically possible and practically feasible.

4.4 Hayek and tacit knowledge

Hayek and the Austrian school developed in their polemic with Neurath a paradigm for the social or moral sciences to the effect that society must be understood in terms of men's conscious reflected actions, it being assumed that people are constantly consciously choosing between different possible courses of action. Any collective phenomena must thus be conceived of as the unintended outcome of the decisions of individual conscious actors.

This imposes a fundamental dichotomy between the study of nature and of society, since in dealing with natural phenomena it may be reasonable to suppose that the individual scientist can know all the relevant information, while in the social context this condition cannot possibly be met. Hence the hostility to the scientism of Neurath.

We believe that Hayek's objection is fundamentally misplaced. Even Laplace, who is famously cited as an advocate of determinism argued that although the universe was in principle predictable to the smallest detail, this was in practice impossible because of limited knowledge and that thus science had to have recourse to probability theory. Certainly since Boltzmann it has been understood how collective phenomena arise as 'unintended' or emergent outcomes of a mass of uncoordinated processes. The recent econophysics literature, for example Farjoun and Machover (1983), Wright (2005) or Yakovenko (2005) shows how the distribution of income under capitalist social relations arises in a similar way. But these authors did not have to model consciousness on the part of the economic actors to get this result. Instead, their application of techniques derived from statistical mechanics to the understanding of the economy, is an exemplary application of Neurath's principle of the unity of science.

In Hayek's view, there were two knowledge forms: scientific knowledge (understood as knowledge of general laws) versus "unorganized knowledge" or "knowledge of the particular circumstances of time and place". The former, he says, may be susceptible of centralization via a "body of suitably chosen experts" (Hayek (1945), p. 521) but the latter is a different matter.

> [P]ractically every individual has some advantage over others in that he possesses unique information of which beneficial use might be made, but of which use can be made only if the decisions depending on it are left to him or are made with his active

cooperation. (Hayek (1945), pp. 521–22)

Hayek is thinking here of "knowledge of people, of local conditions, and special circumstances" (Hayek (1945), p. 522), e.g., of the fact that a certain machine is not fully employed, or of a skill that could be better utilized. He also cites the sort of specific, localized knowledge relied upon by shippers and arbitrageurs. He claims that this sort of knowledge is often seriously undervalued by those who consider general scientific knowledge as paradigmatic.

But this leaves out of account whole layer of knowledge that is crucial for economic activity, namely knowledge of specific technologies, knowledge captured in designs, knowledge captured in software1. Such knowledge is not reducible to general scientific law (it is generally a non-trivial problem to move from a relevant scientific theory to a workable industrial innovation), but neither is it so time- or place-specific that it is non-communicable. The licensing and transfer of technologies in a capitalist context shows this quite clearly. It also misses out the tendency of capitalist society to capture ever more human knowledge in objective form as described by Braverman (1975) or Harris:

> once a worker's knowledge is captured as structural capital, you can then do away with the worker. In industrial capitalism the worker's surplus labor was expropriated, but you had to retain the worker as long as you wanted to make use of his labor. The worker still owned his labor power, and sold it for his wages. But in the new economy, knowledge is both labour and the means of production, both of which are expropriated and turned into structural capital for the exclusive use of the corporation. Thus, intellectual capital can be totally alienated from the worker. Not only is the value of the labor stolen, but the labor itself. Harris (1996)

It would be anachronistic to accuse Hayek of not seeing knowledge in software, but in his day knowledge already existed in the control programs for automatic machines, for instance piano-la rolls. As early as 1948, Vonegut had, in his novel *Player Piano*, given a devastatingly funny critique of these very processes in American capitalism later examined by Braverman. The title of the novel, says it all.

Hayek's notion of knowledge existing solely 'in the mind' is an obstacle to understanding. Let's look at a developed version of Hayek's argument, namely his 1945 article, "The Use of Knowledge in Society". There he distinguishes between knowledge of general principles or rules (easily communicated) and knowledge of "particular circumstances of time and place", which he thought would forever remain dispersed, lodged in the minds of the individuals who alone were in a position to know certain things. This sort of highly specific knowledge, he thought, could not be communicated directly; it could be integrated only via the market mechanism. It is by now all but universal practice for firms to keep records of their inputs and outputs in the form of some sort of computer spreadsheet. These computer files form an image of the firm's input–output characteristics, an image which is readily transferable. Further, even the sort of 'particular' knowledge which Hayek thought too localized to be susceptible to centralization is now routinely centralized. Take his example of the information possessed by shiping clerks.

In the 1970s American Airlines achieved the position of the world's largest airline, to a great extent on the strength of their development of the SABRE system of computerized booking of flights Gibbs (1994). Since then we have come to take it for granted that either we will be able to tap into the Internet to determine where and when there are flights available from just about any A to any B across the world. Hayek's appeal to localized knowledge in this sort of context may have been appropriate at the time of writing, but it is now clearly outdatedd.

Hayek's shipping clerk is long gone, replaced by a relational database that can be accessed easily by anyone with basic computer skills. Or closer to home, think of the travel agent. Once upon a time, we went to travel agents to arrange any but the simplest trip. Now we go online, check a few large, continuously updated databases (Travelocity, Opodo or whatever), compare prices, and buy e-tickets with a credit card.

It might be unfair to fault Hayek for failing to foresee this sort of thing but it's fair to fault his followers in the 21st century for talking as if nothing had changed. Our challenge to those who continue to cite the Austrians is this: please state explicitly what kind of knowledge you're thinking of, that cannot be articulated, communicated, or captured in a computer database, yet is important to the functioning of the economy; please explain how the market is able to integrate this sort of knowledge in the service of the common good; and please explain why a planned system cannot reproduce this effect. (Hayek's own arguments fall a long way short of being demonstrative on the last two questions, even if we grant his point about dispersal of knowledge in the bygone era of shipping clerks.) Hayek's original problem – regarding knowledge that is "specific to time and place" – was a problem that one can easily understand, and also a difficult problem at the time he was writing. If the central planners had to gather and collate information from all those places, using the information technology of the 1940s, before an optimal decision could be made, there is an obvious danger that the information would be seriously out of date before it was available as a guide to decision, with bad economic consequences.

But this particular problem is solved by modern information technology. The Austrian response in terms of "tacit knowledge" represents a retreat from Hayek's formulation of the 1940s. The original problem now being solved, a new problem has to be invented to trip up the socialists.

"Tacit knowledge" has the polemical virtue that it simply can't be communicated to the planning computers, because it can't even be articulated by the person who possesses it, by definition.

Is there such a thing as truly tacit knowledge, and if so what is its economic role?

Consider eBay. Every day people buy and sell thousands of things on eBay that previously would have been put out in the rubbish or left mouldering in attics or cupboards. Why? Because with an online auction service, transactions costs are dramatically lowered. Similarly with very specific knowledge that may be difficult to articulate. You've developed a very particular skill; you'd like to pass it on to others if possible – but how to find someone else who's interested? There may be a nice interaction here: the person who's at a beginner level asks questions of the experienced person, who is then led to articulate his or her knowledge. What we are suggesting is that, to a large extent, "tacit knowledge" may be like "unsaleable goods". Yes, there may be some of both, but both categories have shrunk substantially with easy Internet communication. To repeat a theme from above, tacit knowledge would shrink much further with the abolition of commercial secrecy. People would be free to communicate skills that are now seen as trade secrets of their employers.

What about the hard core of knowledge that really remains tacit?

The tennis player who knows how to launch a serve at 150kph, the violinist how knows how to play a Bach Partita note-perfect and with expression?

To do these things you need the right genetic inheritance, good training, and lots of practice. Why should it a problem for planning?

The Soviet Union had plenty of excellent sportsmen and women, excellent musicians and scientists.

The "tacit knowledge" objection to planning has, in our view, never been stated in a convincing manner. Some knowledge (or skills, really) cannot be codified and transmitted, but we don't see that it's the sort of knowledge that is needed for planning. It's "knowledge" that can be used by those who possess it, in a market system or a planned economy.

Tab. 3: Excess mortality following introduction of Hayekian economics in Russia.

Year	Total Mortality 1000s	Excess Relative to 1986 1000s
1986	1,498.0	0.0
1987	1,531.6	33.6
1988	1,569.1	71.1
1989	1,583.8	85.8
1990	1,656.0	158.0
1991	1,690.7	192.7
1992	1,807.4	309.4
1993	2,129.3	631.3
1994	2,301.4	803.4
1995	2,203.8	705.8
1996	2,082.2	584.2
1997	2,015.8	517.8
1998	1,988.7	490.7
1999	2,144.3	646.3
2000	2,225.3	727.3
2001	2,251.8	753.8

Total Excess Deaths 6,711,200

4.5 Conclusion

Hayek and his followers have grossly overestimated the difficulties of carrying out rational socialist planning. They have coupled this with an exaggerated idea of the effectiveness of the free market as an economic regulator. Their fundamental theoretical errors are:

1. To talk about information in a general and nonquatitative way. This leads them to overestimate how important information about prices is, as compared to other information flows that regulate quantities and qualities of goods.

2. To talk in a vague way about the intractability of socialist calculation, without attempting to be systematic about what these alleged difficulties are. Once one specifies what calculations actually have to be done, one can see that these general objections are without substance.

The coherence of an economy is basically maintained by regular exchanges of *in-natura* information about quatitites in material rather than monetary units. In the USSR these information flows about material units were coordinated through the planning system. Being antagonistic to anything that smacked of Neurath's calculations in kind, the importance of these quatitative measures in economic regulation were systematically underestimated by Hayekians so they failed to anticipate the catastrophic effect of destroying the existing *in-natura* communication system.

The western economists who had criticised the socialist system as inefficient had anticipated that the inauguration of a market economy would lead to accelerated economic growth in the USSR. Instead it regressed from a super-power to an economic basket case. It became dominated by gangsterism. Its industries collapsed and it experienced untold millions of premature deaths, revealed in the statistics of a shocking drop in life expectancy (Table 3).

A discipline less sure of itself than economics, might question its starting hypothesis when an experiment went so drastically wrong. Two of todays leading Hayekians, have instead attempted to use the Searlean distinction between syntax and semantics to explain this signal failure of economic advice Boettke and Subrick (2002). They claim that the shock therapy in the USSR had changed the syntax of the economy but not the semantics:

> "Just because the political structure collapsed, there is no reason to assume that the social structure did. Social arrangements

persisted prior to and after the fall of communism. The reformers and western advisors failed to acknowledge that the newly freed countries were not tabula rasa. They were instead countries that had residents who held beliefs about the world and the structure of society."

These beliefs and attitudes that persisted from socialism are then blamed for the economic collapse. What Boettke and Subrick are attempt to move towards with their syntax/semantics distinction applied to a society is something very like what Marx's distinction between base and superstructure. It might be objected that there was a metaphorical character to this distinction in Marx. So there was. But a century and more of theoretical writings by other Marxists have given a dense social-theoretical content to what were once architectural metaphors. It remains to be seen whether the Austrian school can achieve a similar theoretical development of Boettke's syntax/semantics dichotomy. Marx was concerned from the outset with the historical process of transition between forms of economy - modes of production.

Once the Austrian economists became proponents of social engineering, the very approach Hayek criticised in Neurath, they started to encroach, albeit in reverse gear, a traditional concerns of Marxian economics: transitions between modes of production. But they approached it with a theoretical framework inimical to the object under study. Faced with the manifest failure of their policies they are reduced to metaphors borrowed from linguistics to explain it.

They and the whole Austrian school are unwilling to contemplate the possibility that they were fundamentally wrong in their faith in the organising and communications ability of the market.

References

[1] Andersen, E.D., Gondzio, J., Meszaros, C., Xu, X., 1996, Implementation of interior point methods for large scale linear programming, *Interior Point Methods of Mathematical Programming*, 189–252.

[2] Aristotle, 1962, *The politics*, English translation by T. A. Sinclair, Penguin, London, (Original *circa* 330 **BC**).

[3] Arnold, N. S. 1987. 'Marx and disequilibrium in market socialist relations of production', *Economics and Philosophy*, vol. 3, no. 1, April.

[4] Augustinovics, Maria 1975. 'Integration of mathematical and traditional methods of planning', in Bornstein, M. (ed.) *Economic Planning, East and West*, Cambridge, Mass.: Ballinger.

[5] Bland,R. 1981,*The allocation of Resources by Linear Programming*, Scientific American, June 1981.

[6] Bardhan, P. and Roemer, J. 1992. 'Market socialism: a case for rejuvenation', *Journal of Economic Perspectives*, vol. 6, no. 3, Summer.

[7] Beer, S. 1975. *Platform for Change*, London: Wiley.

[8] Bell, G. 1992. 'Ultracomputers', *Communications of the Association for Computing Machinery*, vol. 35, no. 8, August.

[9] Baker, G. L. and Gollub, J. P.: 1990, Chaotic Dynamics, Cambridge University Press.

[10] Barnsley, M.: 1988, Fractals Everywhere, Academic Press.

[11] Becker, K. H. and Dorfler, M.: 1989, Dynamical Systems and Fractals, Cambridge University Press.

[12] Braverman, H., 1975, Labor and monopoly capital, Monthly Review Press New York.

[13] Bronner, S. E. 1990. *Socialism Unbound*, London: Routledge.

[14] Cockshott, P. 1990. 'Application of artificial intelligence techniques to economic planning', *Future Computer Systems*, vol. 2, no. 4.

[15] Cockshott, W. P. and Cottrell, A. 1989. 'Labour value and socialist economic calculation', *Economy and Society*, vol. 18, no. 1, February.

[16] Cockshott, W. P. and Cottrell, A. 1993. *Towards a New Socialism*, Nottingham: Spokesman Books.

[17] Cottrell, A. and Cockshott, W. P. 1993a. 'Calculation, complexity and planning: the socialist calculation debate once again', *Review of Political Economy*.

[18] Cockshott, W.P, and Cottrell, A., 1994 'Does Marx Need to Transform', *Marxian Economics a Centenary Appraisal*, International Conference on Karl Marx's Third Volume of Capital: 1894-1994, University of Bergamo, December 1994.

[19] Cockshott, W. P., Cottrell, A. and Michaelson, G., 1995, 'Testing Marx: some new results from UK data', forthcoming in *Capital and Class*.

[20] Cockshott, W. P., Cottrell, A. 1997 Labour time versus alternative value bases: a research note. Paul Cockshott, Allin Cottrell, Cambridge Journal of Economics, Vol. 21 No 4, pp. 545-549.

[21] Devine, P. 1988. *Democracy and Economic Planning*, Cambridge: Polity Press.

[22] Djilas, M., 1957, *The new class: an analysis of the communist system*, Frederick A. Praeger, New York.

[23] Ellman, M. 1971. *Soviet Planning Today: Proposals for an Optimally Functioning Economic System*, Cambridge: Cambridge University Press.

[24] Farjoun, E. and Machover, M., 1983, *Laws of Chaos*, London: Verso.

[25] Finley, M. 1985, *Democracy Ancient and Modern*, Hogarth Press, London.

[26] Furr, G., 2005, Stalin and the Struggle for Democratic Reform, *Cultural Logic*, Vol 8., 2005, http://www.clogic.eserver.org/2005/2005.html.

[27] Gibbs, W. W.: 1994, Software's chronic crisis, *Scientific American* 271, 86–95.

[28] Goodman, S. E. and McHenry, W.K. 1986. 'Computing in the USSR: recent progress and policies', *Soviet Economy*, vol. 2, no. 4.

[29] Harris, J.: 1996, From das capital to dos capital: A look at recent theories of value, Technical report, Chicago Third Wave Study Group.

[30] Hayek, F. A.: 1935, Prices and Production, Routledge, London.

[31] Hayek, F. A.: 1945, The use of knowledge in society, *American Economic Review* pp. 519–530.

[32] Hayek, F. A.: 1955, The Counter-Revolution of Science, The Free Press, New York.

[33] Iverson. K. 1979, Notation as a tool of thought. In *ACM Turing award lectures*, page 1979. ACM, New York, NY, USA, 2007.

[34] Kantorovich., LV, 1960, MathematicalMethods of Organizing and Planning Production. *Management Science*, 6(4):366–422.

[35] Kenworthy, L. 1990. 'What kind of economic system? A leftist's guide', *Socialist Review*, vol. 20, no. 2, April–June.

[36] Kotz, D. 1992. 'The direction of Soviet economic reform: from socialist reform to capitalist restoration', *Monthly Review*, vol. 44, no. 4, September.

[37] Kushnirsky, F. I. 1982. *Soviet Economic Planning 1965–1980*, Boulder, Colorado: Westview.

[38] Lange, O. 1938. 'On the economic theory of socialism', in Lippincott, B. (ed.), *On the Economic Theory of Socialism*. New York: McGraw-Hill.

[39] Lange, O. 1967. 'The computer and the market', in Feinstein, C. (ed.), *Socialism, Capitalism and Economic Growth: Essays Presented to Maurice Dobb*, Cambridge: Cambridge University Press.

[40] Lavigne, P., Lavigne, M., 1979, *Regards sur la Constitution sovietique de 1977*, Economica, Collection Politique Compareacutee, Paris .

[41] Lavoie, D. 1985. *Rivalry and Central Planning*, Cambridge: Cambridge University Press.

[42] Levine, A. 1984. *Arguing for Socialism*, London: Routledge & Kegan Paul.

[43] Mandel, E. 1986. 'In defence of socialist planning', *New Left Review*, no. 159, Sept–Oct.

[44] Mandel, E. 1988. 'The myth of market socialism', *New Left Review*, no. 169, May–June.

[45] Mandel, E. 1991. 'The roots of the present crisis in the Soviet economy', in Miliband, R. and Panitch, L. (eds), *The Socialist Register 1991*, London: Merlin.

[46] Marx, K. 1875, *Critique of the Gotha Programme* , People's Publishing House Peking, 1972.

[47] Marx, K. 1972. *Capital*, Volume 3, London: Lawrence and Wishart.

[48] Marx, K. 1976. *Capital*, Volume 1, Harmondsworth: Penguin/New Left Review.

[49] Miller, D. 1989. *Market, State and Community: Theoretical Foundations of Market Socialism*, Oxford: Clarendon Press.

[50] Mises, L. von 1935: 'Economic calculation in the socialist commonwealth', in von Hayek, F. A., (ed.) *Collectivist Economic Planning*, London: Routledge & Kegan Paul.

[51] Mises, L. von 1951. *Socialism*, New Haven: Yale University Press.

[52] Murrell, P. 1983. 'Did the theory of market socialism answer the challenge of Ludwig von Mises? A reinterpretation of the socialist controversy', *History of Political Economy* 15, 92–105.

[53] von Neumann. J., 1945, A Model of General Economic Equilibrium. *Review of Economic Studies*, 13(33):1–9.

[54] Neurath. O., 1917, The Conceptual Structure of Economic Theory and its Foundations. In Thomas Uebel and Robert Cohen, editors, *Economic Writings*. Kluwer, (1917) 2004.

[55] Neurath. O., 1919 Economics in Kind, Calculation in Kind and their Relation to War Economics. In Thomas Uebel and Robert Cohen, editors, *Economic Writings*. Kluwer, (1919) 2004.

[56] Nove, A. 1977. *The Soviet Economic System*, London: George Allen and Unwin.

[57] Nove, A. 1983. *The Economics of Feasible Socialism*, London: George Allen and Unwin.

[58] Ochoa, E. M., 1989, 'Values, prices, and wage–profit curves in the US economy', *Cambridge Journal of Economics*, vol. 13, no. 3, September, pp. 413–29.

[59] Petrovic, P., 1987, 'The deviation of production prices from labour values: some methodology and empirical evidence', *Cambridge Journal of Economics*, vol. 11, no. 3, September, pp. 197–210.

[60] Przeworski, A. 1989. 'Class, production and politics: A reply to Burawoy', *Socialist Review*, vol. 19, no. 2, April–June.

[61] Pugh, W. et al, *IBM's 360 and Early 370 Systems*, MIT Press, Massachusetts Institute of Technology, Cambridge, 1991.

[62] R. Remak. Kann die Volkswirtschaftslehre eine exakteWissenschaft werden, *Jahrbücher für Nationalökonomie und Statistik*, 131:703–735, 1929.

[63] Rodbertus, K. 1904. *Das Kapital*,Griard and Brière, 1904.

[64] Shaikh, A. M.: 1998, The empirical strength of the labour theory of value, in R. Bellofiore (ed.), Marxian Economics: A Reappraisal, Vol. 2, Macmillan, pp. 225– 251.

[65] Shaikh, A., 1984, 'The transformation from Marx to Sraffa', in A. Freeman and E. Mandel (eds) *Ricardo, Marx, Sraffa*, London: Verso, pp. 43–84.

[66] Smolinski, L. (ed.) 1977. *L.V. Kantorovich: Essays in Optimal Planning*, Oxford: Basil Blackwell.

[67] Stalin, J. V. 1952. *Economic Problems of Socialism in the USSR*, New York: International Publishers.

[68] Stalin, J. V. 1955. *Works*, Volume 12, Moscow: Foreign Languages Publishing House.

[69] Strumilin, S. G. 1977. 'K teorii tsenoobrazovaniya v usloviyakh sotsializma', in Akademiya Nauk USSR, editors, *Aktual'niye problemy ekonomicheskoy nauki v trudakh S. G. Strumilina*, Moscow: Nauka.

[70] Temkin, G. 1989. 'On Economic reforms in socialist countries: the debate on economic calculation under socialism revisited', *Communist Economies* 1, 31–59.

[71] Treml, V. 1967. 'input–output analysis and Soviet planning', in Hardt, J. P. (ed.), *Mathematics and computers in Soviet economic planning*, New Haven: Yale University Press.

[72] Treml, V. 1989. 'The most recent Soviet input–output table: a milestone in Soviet statistics', *Soviet Economy*, vol. 5, no. 4.

[73] Tretyakova, A. and Birman, I. 1976. 'input–output analysis in the USSR', *Soviet Studies*, vol. XXVIII, no. 2, April.

[74] Trotsky, L., 2004, *The Revolution Betrayed*, Dover Publications.

[75] Valle Baeza, A., 1994, 'Correspondence between labor values and prices: a new approach', *Review of Radical Political Economics*, vol. 26, no. 2, pp. 57–66.

[76] Wright, I.: 2005, The social architecture of capitalism, Physica A: *Statistical Mechanics and its Applications* 346(3-4), 589–620.

[77] Yakovenko, V.M., Silva, A.C., 2005, Two-class structure of income distribution in the USA: Exponential bulk and power-law tail, *Econophysics of Wealth Distributions*, Springer, pp.15–23.

[78] Yun, O. 1988. *Improvement of Soviet Economic Planning*, Moscow: Progress Publishers.

[79] Zachariah. D, 2006, Labour value and equalisation of profit rates. Indian Development Review, 4(1):1–21.

Printed in Great Britain
by Amazon.co.uk, Ltd.,
Marston Gate.